So You Want to Buy a Small Hotel!

...and what a parking place!

So You Want to Buy a Small Hotel!

A Guide

Joanne Muller
Edited by
Charles Humphrey Muller

Writers Club Press
San Jose New York Lincoln Shanghai

So You Want to Buy a Small Hotel!
A Guide

All Rights Reserved © 2001 by Joanne Muller

No part of this book may be reproduced or transmitted in any form or by any means, graphic, electronic, or mechanical, including photocopying, recording, taping, or by any information storage retrieval system, without the permission in writing from the publisher.

Writers Club Press
an imprint of iUniverse.com, Inc.

For information address:
iUniverse.com, Inc.
5220 S 16th, Ste. 200
Lincoln, NE 68512
www.iuniverse.com

Cartoon illustrations by Fred Ohnewald

ISBN: 0-595-20095-8

Printed in the United States of America

Dedication

To all our wonderful and loving guests–to our German Drinkers (Fred and Christiane) who intoxicated us with their friendship and raspberry schnapps and rendered us incapable of serving breakfasts with our balloon heads; to Cyril and the lads with their annual pilgrimage to St Andrews; to Jan our doctor friend whom we found doing the Highland Fling in the dining room before breakfast; to Wendy and Gordon in their annual trek to their remote Highland cottage; to Miss Vertue who never complained about being put in the attic and who never forgot the children; to Avril and Judith who engaged us in endless conversions and tested our literary knowledge; to the Kays who beguiled us with their botanical expertise; to the Kings with their charm and wit; to Derek Marshall and Sarge (who kept law and order) and the rest of the Welsh choir; to Charles Elliott from California and his running togs, and to Denise Elliott whom we mistook for his daughter; to Mr Maxwell with his stentorian voice and who found it hard to say goodbye; to Bruce and Kirsty Lockhart with their Christian fellowship; to Mr & Mrs Ledger who engaged us in more endless conversation; to yotties John and Esther Livingston with their seafaring expertise; to the charming Dr Chittie and his enchanting wife who introduced us to new styles in painting; to Stephen and Elaine who brightened many a New Year's eve; to Murray and Elizabeth who traveled all the way from Mull to take care of the hotel while we went on holiday, and to all the rest, far, far too many to mention by name.

Charles & Jo

Contents

Dedication v
Foreword ix
Preface xi

CHAPTER 1
    First Things First 1

CHAPTER 2
    Buying Your Small Hotel 7

CHAPTER 3
    Of Tourist Boards and Advertising! 27

CHAPTER 4
    All that luvelly lolly! So what can I charge? 50

CHAPTER 5
    Reservations: taking bookings and registering guests 60

CHAPTER 6
    Fodder—feeding the herd! Breakfast 68

CHAPTER 7
    Dinners (the easy way!)—Bar (hic!) 77

CHAPTER 8
    The Kitchen—where it all happens! 94

CHAPTER 9
    To sleep, perchance to dream—or in plain English, Bedrooms! 99

CHAPTER 10
    The epitome of boredom—Bookkeeping! 109

CHAPTER 11
    Repeat Trade—Knowing you got it right! 118

CHAPTER 12
    From Strength to Strength: Refurbishment, Development & Expansion! 125

CHAPTER 13
Competitors or allies? *139*
CHAPTER 14
Pernicious Allsorts *142*
CHAPTER 15
So do I really want a small hotel?
(A few good reasons to make you think again!) *154*
CHAPTER 16
The Ideal Hotel *163*
CHAPTER 17
Typical seven days! *166*
CONCLUSIONS *175*
About the Author *177*
Appendix *179*

Foreword

Buying a small hotel in the Scottish Borders was a considerable adventure—and took considerable courage, for hitherto I had enjoyed a secure income as a full professor at a university in South Africa! First of all, Joanne and I had more or less had to smuggle our meager funds out of Apartheid South Africa, since that regime, no doubt sensing its demise, had effectively blocked the transfer of funds out of the country. We used every available opportunity to transfer our funds, bit by bit, whether by travel allowances, gift allowances, or by swopping our salary cheques with British people living in South Africa and being paid in the UK!

In the end, with the help of a mammoth mortgage, we managed to get enough together to buy the Rosebank Hotel in Dedburgh, which gave us a marvelous lifestyle for eleven years, including many exotic holidays, the highlight being a six-week cruise to Australia and a campervan journey across the Australian outback. The mortgage was repaid after four years, and offshoots of the business was the acquisition of two self-catering cottages, now sold. A full account of our venture is given in my book *Have Anything You Really Really Want: A Christian Testimony*, also published by Writers Club Press.

So You Want to Buy a Small Hotel is written with humor and tells it like it is, warts and all, the good things *and* the nightmares about running a hotel—the dream (with the nightmares!) we lived for 11 years at the Rosebank Hotel!

There are times when, living in the Great Glen of the Scottish Highlands, the hotel still comes to mind. Good times—such as those waking moments at 7 a.m. when I realize, with sheer joy, that I *don't* have to get up, put on a bright face and serve breakfasts! Or the now rare times when the phone rings and the person on the line is someone I actually know, a daughter or a friend, and not a guest wanting a non-smoking en-suite bedroom with a view of the Abbey and, please, could he bring his Great Dane? (The tranquility of the phone *not* ringing off the hook is indescribable!) Then there are the frequent times in summer when, on a mountain bike on a track overlooking a vista of lochs and mountains, or on a boat chugging across the placid surface of a sea loch, when the sense of freedom at the height of the tourist season is overwhelming–for one of the greatest disadvantages about running a hotel is that it becomes your prison, unless you can afford staff to liberate you from a hands-on drudgery. Undoubtedly, running the hotel was a good experience, but now that it's gone—man, is life good, not getting up *every* morning, weekdays and weekends, at 7 to cook and serve breakfasts, then to clean rooms, to have the phone or the doorbell ringing persistently, having guests arrive prematurely, almost as soon as the previous lot have checked out. Do I miss it? I guess so—like a hole in the head! (I guess some of the negative experiences overflowed into my novel *Continental Drift*, or the second volume of *Wheel of Fortune* where I devoted an entire chapter to the admittedly few guests who got under my skin! On a more positive note, the hotel *did* provide me with the time to write a few books, including novels; but then that's largely due to my loving and longsuffering wife who was kind enough to man–or 'woman'–the phone and doorbell, and attend to guests when they rang the cowbell to say their shower didn't work, to ask where the car park was, to ask how to turn on the TV, to ask if they could buy one of the placemats as a souvenir, to ask for dinner, or a drink, or for change for the payphone. Just a few unpleasant guests can rankle in the memory and make it seem like things were always bad–whereas, in fact, 99.9% of them were marvelous and a few have actually taken the trouble to come and see us here in the Great Glen!)

Want to buy and run a small hotel? Sure, it's great–go for it! But you just *may* want to think again.

Charles Humphrey Muller, MA (Wales),
PhD (Lond), DLitt (OFS), DEd (SA)

Preface

We bought some shares in a diamond mine recently and the blurb in one of the financial magazines said 'not for the faint-hearted.' In so many ways that could apply to the hotel business!

Some people *fall* into the hotel business through redundancy, some the need to earn a little more towards life's little luxuries (otherwise known as pin money). Some to retire! Some just think it would be fun. To others it's a vocation.

We didn't altogether 'fall' into it. We had considered it many years ago but then it got put onto the back burner. However, thirteen years ago we returned from living in South Africa with most of our money whittled away by a dwindling exchange rate. We investigated many business ideas, taking into account our young family, our interests and qualifications. Charles had left a good position as Professor and Head of an English Department at a university in South Africa. I had been a housewife for such a long time that this was my only 'qualification,' apart from office skills long forgotten.

We looked at franchises and came very close to joining one or two (we actually gave one our deposit twice and bailed out at the last moment); but the fact that we had to share our hard-earned money with a franchisor sort of got to us. Some of the franchises we looked at have actually gone bust and so has one of the businesses we'd considered. When we look back we realize we made the right choice. The Rosebank Hotel has been a good little business, not intellectually challenging, but it gave us a secure income for eleven years and the place is in much better shape than when we bought it in 1990. And in spite of the occasional frustrations, it has certainly rewarded us with a lifestyle that many salaried nine-to-five folk might envy! We have since sold the hotel and moved to the Scottish

Highlands, but the book itself–the text that follows–was written while we were still *in situ* and in close contact with the day-to-day running of the business.

I've tried in this book to give a truthful account of *how it is—or how it was!—for us*. One has to be realistic, of course. After all, even roses have thorns. No pain, no gain! Hopefully, after reading this you'll have a clearer idea of what it's really like and whether running a small hotel is for you.

Joanne Muller

The Rosebank Hotel–a drawing by Carol Bathgate

CHAPTER 1

First Things First

When I told people I was going to buy my own hotel I was surprised by the different reactions—from 'Gosh, you're going to make a lot of money' to 'You must be mad! That's *terribly* hard work!'

All I knew at the time was that I was desperate to get out of the rat race. I was sick and tired of working for a boss for a weekly wage that was a mere pittance. I was tired of scraping the barrel every week, trying to make ends meet. When my husband got a teaching job, he was exhausted by the hours spent commuting in the dark. One day a collision with another car cost him his entire month's salary.

Well, I *did* buy a small hotel and it didn't cost me an arm and a leg! Selling my small three-bedroomed house in Harrogate gave me enough money to put down as a deposit on a small six-bedroomed hotel in the Scottish Borders. One thing I can certainly tell you after eight years of trading: it revolutionized my lifestyle, *and* definitely for the better! Instead of a salary I have a cashflow that's given me everything I want: a comfortable home, a Mercedes Benz, clothing and food for me and my family, and each year a fantastic holiday in places like the Canary Islands, Malta, Barbados, not to mention a cruise to Australia. In the meantime I've bought and sold two holiday cottages and paid off the £65,000 commercial mortgage on the hotel.

And yet, although I have owned my hotel for ten years, it sometimes feels like a lifetime! I hope that by reading this book you'll not only have a good idea of how to run your own hotel but also whether or not you actually *want* to own one!

Perhaps it would be a good idea to elaborate on the main advantages of having your own small hotel. Try these for starters:

1. It's true, you *can* escape the Rat Race! No more standing in a crowd or in the train/underground/bus on your way to work! No more sitting fuming in your car on a cold and misty morning while the traffic queues grow bigger and bigger. Ice, snow, rain—it doesn't matter. You just hop out of bed, fall down the stairs and hey presto!—you're there, at work. You may even get an extra hour in bed compared to what you have now. I rise at 7.30 a.m. I'll bet a lot of you rise earlier than me!

2. Forget the winter blues—that's if your hotel is seasonal like mine. My husband and I just *love* winter. Winter is our time off—time to relax, indulge in a hobby like painting, and take a package holiday to the sun.

Most people have weekends off and a fortnight's holiday once a year. With a seasonal hotel you have much more time off. You can really get your teeth into your hobby. Go for walks, read, write, paint—whatever takes your fancy. (Both my husband and I paint and we've filled the walls of the public rooms with our oil paintings, many of which are bought by guests during the season.)

You could even have a small apartment somewhere nice and warm and disappear for those nasty winter months. It's cheaper to stay somewhere warm (like Malta or the Canaries) and you can let the apartment out to pay for itself in the summer. Indulge yourself! Hey, you could even hibernate!

3. Forget that Monday-morning feeling. (In a sense, *every* day is Monday—or whatever other day of the week you choose to make it!) It's *your* business so Mondays, as such, don't exist.

4. You're dealing with happy people (this should appeal to doctors and dentists)! The chances are you will be buying a hotel for tourists and people are generally happy on holiday—with the possible exception of Americans who can be aggressive consumers and can take their holidays too seriously!

5. You're working for yourself. YOU are in control of your own destiny. The world's your oyster, the sky's the limit. Once you've tasted the pleasure of being your own boss you'll never work for anyone ever again. You can give reign to your entrepreneurial skill and forge from strength to strength, or you can be laid back and limp along as long as you make enough to make ends meet. The chances are you're not the latter since—yes, running a hotel *is* hard work.

6. Your business comes to you. Your car can stay in the garage. The weather can do what it likes. Cut down on motoring expenses—even sell the car!

7. There is no hard sell. On the whole people *want* to stay. You don't have to phone them and cajole them into staying—they phone you!

8. There are no debts. People pay up front.

9. A small hotel can be a wonderful stepping-stone and secure base for starting a new home-based business such as mail order or even enabling a hobby you have always fancied mushrooming into a business of its own. The telephone is at hand. You're there all the time in the season to work at a second business for a few hours a day and get more out of it in the winter when time is your own. Phasing in a business this way certainly cuts the risks, since you're already earning a living from the hotel while the other gets off the ground.

You would cut down on expenses such as traveling, expensive premises, and overheads like insurance and electricity. You could start a taxi service, a health club in a spare room (convert the garage if you sell the car), an employment agency, a video club, or a dating agency! If your new hobby/business is preferable to the hotel, then you could phase it in as you phase out the hotel aspect. (The hotel business has given my husband the opportunity of becoming a writer: he writes poetry and novels, and the hotel guests stimulate his ideas for characters!)

10. Owning your own hotel affords you the opportunity to live in a beautiful part of the country—somewhere where you've always fancied living, whether it be the Lake District or the Isle of Harris, provided it's a good catchment area for guests. You could live in the city center, if that's what you prefer. Isn't there somewhere you've always had a hankering to live but couldn't get a job there?

11. Your children are taken care of since you're always at hand to see to them. No more 'latch key' kids. Coming home to an empty house while mum and dad are working can be a desolate thing for a young child.

*   *   *

It's amazing how many of our guests say, "This looks like fun. We wouldn't mind a little B&B. Do you think *we* could do it?"

Anyone can do it. Read on and see if *you* want to do it!

CHAPTER 2

Buying Your Small Hotel

Assuming the previous chapter's 'eleven good reasons' for buying piqued your interest, then the next thing is to look at properties held by estate agents to get an idea of prices and what's available.

In Britain there are quite a few hotel agents who cover the whole country, such as Robert Barry and Christies. You'll find them in the address section at the back. Give them a ring and ask for their catalogue of hotels and guesthouses or pubs. This will give you a good general view of size and prices. If you see anything you like, ask for the sale particulars. Catering magazines like *The Caterer, Licensee* and *Freehouse* (the two latter are sent to me free by Freehouse, address in back) also publish advertisements placed by agents selling hotels.

There are many websites on the Internet that feature hotels and guesthouses, or B&Bs, for sale. Christies, Robert Barry, and Knight Frank, all have their websites, but a very useful one is *www.buyahotel.co.uk*.

If you are looking specifically in your area there should be agents locally who will also deal with hotels and guesthouses. Look in *The Yellow Pages* and give them a ring. Some agents specialize in businesses.

Having found a few businesses that really appeal to you, then mess about with some figures first. Do your own cashflow forecast to make sure you can afford what you're looking at. The large agents will give some advice on this. You may be able to afford a bigger place than you imagine. It depends on turnover and profits. In our own case we underestimated the outgoings when we came into the business. It's amazing how much goes out compared with what comes in! We made 55% profit last year but that was only because we didn't spend much on the business; and if you want to keep in shape you have to spend a bit every year. You can generally only see the business books after the viewing.

The size of your mortgage will be the most important factor. I've done a very basic cashflow/outgoings forecast for a year to give you an idea of what you can expect from a small guest house with six double bedrooms that trades for say eight months of the year up to the present VAT level of £50,000 with no staff. Remember, you don't have to pay a stamp for staff if they earn less than £81 a week (check with your local Tax Office) so it might pay to use a couple of part-timers if you don't want a lot of help. Here is the forecast:

Probable outgoings of an establishment with six letting bedrooms

(Assuming you're staying out of VAT and that the present level is £50,000 over a rolling twelve month period.)

Takings:

    Accommodation. 40,500

    Food. *5,500*

    (Don't bite the VAT level on the nose!). 46,000

Overheads

    Food & bar (you will have eaten out of this). 5,100

    Rates. 1,500

    Insurance. 750

Your mortgage

    Repairs & replacements. 1,600

    Property repairs 500

    Heat & light. 2,500

    Cleaning 500

    TV licence. 92

    Stationery & post 180

    Advertising 2,400

    Telephone. 700

    Car—travelling. 1,000

    Subscriptions 200

Legal & prof.—accounting 700
Sundries 1,500
Bank interest
Loan interest
HP interest
Leasing charges (phone, machines)
Depreciation—vehicles 300
Depreciation—fixtures & fittings *1,000*
20,522
46,000
-20,522
Net profit for the year *24,478*

Bear in mind that you'll have lived off this—e.g. food, electricity, loo rolls, everything in fact that you would have bought to keep a normal house going. You must add your own mortgage repayments, pension, insurance and other private outgoings. Maybe you intend to use the car a lot, in which case you'll have larger expenses. You may have to spend quite a lot on refurbishment at first, in which case Property Repairs will be higher (but remember this is tax deductible). Alter the above to suit your needs and the needs of the place you have under review.

Obviously tailoring your cashflow exactly at this stage would be impossible until you see the books of the place you would like to purchase. The takings are generally mentioned in the sale particulars.

Capital

I think you'll find that Building Societies don't give mortgages on hotels any more. Rather try one of the major banks. They are used to dealing with new small businesses and many offer business packs and have special small business advisors. I found Nat West particularly useful when I was enquiring about a different business to this. As a general rule a Bank will give up to two times your own investment, subject to a convincing cash-flow forecast. If you're prepared to commit then they are too!

Business loans are flexible and each Bank will let you know how they prefer to deal with their repayments. Obviously if you have youth on your side, your loan can be for longer and your monthly repayments less. If you're too young of course then they may take more persuading. If you're too old they won't want to know! I can never work out what the best age is! Rates can be fixed, variable or at a monthly managed rate. Maybe your bank can arrange interest-free banking for the first year. Obviously you'll have to pay for it in the end but just to get you up and started it can be very handy.

Shop around for free banking. My Bank used to offer free banking for the first year of a new business. Bank charges can mount up—they even charge for putting cash in—so free banking makes a lot of sense. Go from bank to bank to assess how much 'clout' you have. Remember, *you* are the customer.

Although money isn't quite so 'available' as it was a few years back banks are usually pleased to see new customers coming in their door and should welcome you. I had to bottle-feed my new-born infant during one bank interview but they were still happy to give me the money I wanted! Most have business guides. Lloyds have a guide which is great but it costs about £15—trust a bank! Above all be professional, or appear to be professional.

Provide them with well thought-out forecasts, a copy for them and the sale particulars. Be conservative (moderation in all things!).

So, you've done your business plan/forecast. The bank likes it. You can afford it. Fantastic! This is going to be a great journey. Give the agent a ring and make an appointment to go and inspect. The best way of doing this is actually staying at the place under review. I'm not sure if this is normal but we did it three times and were pleased we did. Even if we didn't buy the places! It gives you a better 'feel' for the area. Ask about schools and local services. Assess whether it is really the place for you.

If you're looking to buy a dwelling house (or already have a house) to convert into an hotel or B & B and have a mortgage or lease you will need to examine the terms of the agreement to make sure you'll be allowed to carry on a business in the premises. Better to check at the outset.

Going places

Our first visit was to a small hotel in Wales. It was a pretty place overlooking a quiet bay. At first glance it was just what we wanted—sort of 'nooky' and homely. We took a walk into the village in the evening and found the locals were not particularly pleased to see us. There was a very strange mix of atmosphere. This was enough to put us off. If they're unfriendly to visitors then what will they be like with newcomers, not to mention prospective guests to the hotel? On a more personal level, how will my children be treated at the local school?

We then hightailed it off to Scotland to a region that turned out to be a somewhat depressed area and thank God we *didn't* buy there. The brochure showed a wonderful building (beware, photos can be very misleading!). The front of the hotel that overlooked the sea was a mess—something the sale particulars omitted to mention. We didn't expect perfection, of course, since most places will need something doing to them. However, having spent the night in a very mediocre room which certainly needed 'doing up' we were starting to have second thoughts. What turned the tide for me was a visit to the house of horrors early in the morning. I'm not a large person, though I was six months pregnant at the time, but I'm sure this was not the reason for the floor giving way as I sat on the loo. I had hardly settled when I sensed the loo tipping slightly leftwards towards the bath where a black void was opening beside me, the loo and me slowly sinking into more inky blackness threatening to envelop the two of us at any moment. The void got larger and larger, unknown horrors lurking below. In mid-flow I jumped up, waddled (tights still around my knees) towards the door. I still have wonderful bladder control!

It's silly what can put one off a place. I still wonder what was down there! On the other hand I once stayed at a guesthouse near Aviemore, not quite right for us because it was too small—but it had a lovely atmosphere and I would have loved it. The atmosphere is very important, for if you can feel it the guests will too (although guests can bring their own atmosphere with them!). The owner of this hotel was very obliging and drove me to my next appointment—a medium-sized hotel a few miles out of town.

So you see, staying at the place can be a good idea. Even if it's just to put you off! You'll have to pay for the room, of course. If you can't stay, and it won't always be convenient, then at least have a pot of tea in the local tea-room and ask pertinent nosy questions about the hotel in question. See what sort of reputation it has.

The main thing is to have a good look round. Ideally the owners will allow you the opportunity to have a good look round on your own so you can pay more attention to signs of woodworm, wet patches and the like. (A surveyor's report will eventually reveal all the faults, of course, but you may want to dismiss a property on the basis of your own observations before paying a surveyor.) Take your time and make notes for its amazing how quickly one forgets things and one's memory of one hotel merges with that of another.

Feel the beds. Are they worn out? Are the carpets becoming threadbare? You need to bear in mind when viewing a place that not everything is old and worn out. We had to replace just about every single thing, from washing machine to duvets. It can be costly. The pillowcases cost £14 each! If you want a change for each bed, then that's £392 just in pillow cases for a six-bedroomed establishment, not to mention the duvet covers, sheets, pillows etc. Keep your eyes peeled.

These may seem little points when buying, but the cost of replacing essentials really mounts up.

We were very naive when we chose our hotel, for we were desperate to put our roots down, what with one small child and a new baby. It was a buyer's market and we could have held out for longer—but we didn't. We've made the best of what seemed a bad job but the hotel has nevertheless proved to be a thriving little business. We are still here and charging reasonable prices while all around us others have been floundering. Thank heavens—our little hotel was perhaps meant for us after all.

There was so much to replace at first that we spread the costs by using a lot of catalogue items, paying by monthly installments.

It can take a while to find the place just for you. Your criteria will be different to ours. It was essential for us that we had private family accommodation since we had two small children. So many places don't have private suites. We had some friends in the business that shared their lounge with the guests: the alternative was to sit in the kitchen! I wouldn't do that.

You've got to have somewhere where you can escape from the guests or you'll never have any peace. Even when you're out of sight they'll still want you for various—often petty—requirements, like fresh milk or a hair dryer; frequently, it's just to ask a question about the area, or to make light conversation (guests occupying single rooms can be notoriously lonely and will do their best to monopolize your company). Nevertheless, having that door between you makes all the difference to maintaining your sanity!

If you can't afford to replace things at first then consider leasing. Equipment like commercial tumble dryers are expensive. Make sure you work the cost of leasing into your cashflow.

Back to the snooping. Flush the loos (make a note of things that don't work well and should be fixed before you take over). Try the taps. Check that the shower trays or handbasins aren't chipped or cracked. What do the furnishings in the lounge and dining room look like? Are things looking careworn? Any cracks in the walls? Does the whole place need redecorating?

You generally get what you pay for, but beware. There's always someone out there asking for more money than a place is worth. Just because an agent has a place on at a certain price doesn't mean it's worth it.

Ask questions. Look at the bookings chart and see what last year's bookings were like and what the future bookings hold. Mind you, looking at our future bookings won't help a great deal. I'm writing this in May and our bookings average out at 50% full. In full season we will be turning people away even if the bookings had been 20% full. Nevertheless, few or no bookings don't auger a good and productive season!

Consider where the current owners are advertising. Do some sums to make sure that what they are saying adds up to what their accounts say. Have they organized their advertising for the next season? This is normally done a year in advance.

We had some friends who bought a small hotel and were told the turnover was £38,000 (this was ten years ago). Yet in their first year they took only £18,000—and that was *after* they'd done the place up and done extra advertising. Did the previous owners take a lot of business with them? Were they moving locally *or* did they 'doctor' the books for selling? This is not unheard of. So, a wee bit of detective work on the seller's books won't go amiss. You'll be able to get a set of accounts from the agent after you've viewed the place. Watch out for discrepancies. For instance, if they say they're nearly always full but don't spend any money on advertising, then where are the customers coming from? Simple things like that. It's common sense and logic, really. They say they do a lot of dinners, yet their food outgoings aren't as much as you'd expect. Remember, if they have a large family they'll also be eating out of the books. Do a calculation to check that the turnover could feasibly be what the books *say* it is. For example, if they charge £40 a room, then 40 x (say 5 rooms) = £200 a day x 7 days a week = £1400 x 4 weeks = £5,200 a month or whatever. Ask to see their booking chart and see if they did what they said they did! Some unscrupulous people may hike up the turnover to make the place more saleable. Have an accountant look over their books. Don't forget you're paying for goodwill as well as fixtures and stock.

Ask what they are leaving. All the furniture? Most of the equipment? When you decide to buy, ask for an inventory and check it when you move in. We were missing a freezer (you may laugh but we hadn't noticed at first!). Check they leave good linen—if that's what was there when you looked around the place. Are there enough towels, is there enough cutlery, plates? Have they left you with a load of rubbish? Some unscrupulous people may try to swap things before you arrive—the odd deep fryer or microwave may suddenly have taken on ten years since you last saw it at the viewing. Our vendors kept coming back for things they'd 'forgotten.' How very convenient! Take note of the makes of things. Don't trust anyone! Just because you'd never consider cheating someone doesn't mean everyone else is of the same ilk.

Location

Location is the most important thing to bear in mind. When we inspected our prospective hotel on a Sunday we thought it was perfect—just off the main A road, but on a quiet street. It turned out we have a huge housing estate and two factories up the hill from us, so more often than not there is a continuous weekday flow of noisy traffic. It was our own fault—we never thought to look.

And we thought it was a quiet backwater!

You can see us from the main road but we have a major tourist attraction on the other side of this road and people are so busy looking at our beautiful abbey they don't see us till it's too late!

Still, you do need to be close to a main road, if possible in the line of sight from the driver's position—unless you're so unique that people will want to trek down minor roads to find you. I would be as close to a main route as possible, though preferably a touch off it since I don't like main roads. Bit of a contradiction. I'm perhaps not 'money minded' enough.

mportant. The easier you are to find the more customers you'll have. If people can't find you quickly then they'll go to the place on the way to you. So, you don't want to be at the end of a cul-de-sac of guesthouses and you don't want to be in an unlikely place like the middle of a housing estate.

On the whole you're better off being in a town or village unless you have lots of facilities to offer the trapped guest. Some people love to be out in the countryside but from experience I've found the preference is for a place near the pubs and eating houses where the car can be left at the hotel. Some people are incredibly lazy and even take their car into town from us which is five minutes' walk away. They may as well be out in the country since they are using their car anyway. Be within easy walking distance from the amenities, pubs, restaurants, etc.

Take into account competition. Avoid what we call the 'Scarborough syndrome' (or 'Blackpool syndrome'), unless you like that sort of thing. Don't go for a place in a row of other guesthouses, especially at a seaside resort, unless that's where you've always wanted to live, since trade is highly seasonal and highly competitive. You'll have to keep your prices right down to compete and give your meals away. You'll work like a slave for very little. Honestly, it will wear you out. We had considered a resort location, thinking it would be fun—but seeing the faces of those poor worn out guest-house owners made us realize that we cared more for ourselves than that. Having to do dinners for free just to get the bed and breakfast trade is a trap. You'll be up early in the morning and hardly stop till late at night. Really, I wouldn't do it, unless it really appeals to you, or you have staff of course.

You perhaps need to ponder over whether you want a seasonal business or not, whether you want to work like a fiend for about six months of the year to grab your business while you can or whether you'd rather take it a *little* easier with a business that runs a full twelve months.

You don't *have* to buy a going concern, although a proven business with accounts is the safest route to take. You could set up in your own home if it is suitable, or just buy a house and trade from it. Check the local council is happy about it (they may want to look around) and remember that equipment will cost a bit and you can't trade over six people unless you go the whole hog with fire equipment and pay extra rates. Any more than six bed spaces is treated as a ratable business and has legal obligations, apart from requiring a fire certificate. Not declaring yourself as a business is illegal.

Survey

If you're serious about a place then, for goodness sake, get a survey done. Surveys may seem costly but in fact are never as bad as expected and worth every penny. In fact, if you're borrowing for a mortgage then you'll have to get a survey anyway for the Bank. If there is anything wrong with the property then the surveyor should spot it.

The surveyor will be looking for obvious as well as hidden defects that you may have missed on your way round, like dry rot. Our surveyor couldn't get to see one of the guest rooms. He was told by the previous owners that a guest was in the room but that the room was fine. I can't believe we fell for it! We took the owners at their word. (We're still naive and still trust too many people but are developing a crusty shell.) The room in question smelled of damp the moment we opened the door. It didn't require an experienced surveyor to spot the trouble. Inside a built-in cupboard we found the ceiling was soaking wet. The roof needed mending—and it was a costly repair.

The surveyor will check for cracks in walls, roof for old tiles and nail sickness (a condition where the nails holding the tiles in place are so rusted that their heads come off easily, allowing the tiles to slip—a common problem!), and the wood for woodworm—a whole host of things which you should know about before you give your money away. He will probably be local so he should know if the building has an odd sort of reputation. You're paying him so phone and ask if you have any queries about his report.

Go back and look at the place as many times as you feel is necessary. You're the prospective buyer and if the vendor wants to sell and he's confident then he should be happy to oblige.

Law

Remember the law regarding buying in Scotland is different to England and Wales. In Scotland the main thing to bear in mind is that you don't put in an offer and not be prepared to go ahead with it. There's no going back once you've said 'yes.' The offer is made by a solicitor who knows all the legal niceties. He will also check that the property being sold has all the necessary planning permission for improvements or alterations that may have been made. (In Scotland it is the vendor's responsibility to present proof of planning permission for alterations made prior to the sale in the form of building certificates.)

If you are going to sell alcohol then let your solicitor guide you regarding licensing laws. He should check the licence on the property you are buying is up to date. It's a simple thing keeping the licence (see chapter 14). Just keep the place out of trouble, keep it clean (see chapter 14) and make sure electrical appliances the guests use are safe and that your fire certificate is up to date.

Our licence is 'Restricted' meaning for residents only. It's the easiest to get and keep providing you don't break the rules!

Dealing with a new solicitor—especially in Scotland—can be tricky and if you have someone recommended then that's wonderful. We found our solicitor in the Edinburgh Yellow Pages. I think this man made most of his money by keeping me on the phone telling me how wonderful he was. He actually set a clock when he started a conversation on the phone. He thought he was a wheeler dealer and lost the first hotel we really wanted. We were prepared to pay the asking price but he said it was too much and he'd get them down. We thought 'who are we to question someone who obviously knows better than us lowly public.' His offers were so unrealistic that they were refused time and again. It was embarrassing. After endless ingratiating and listening to him sounding his own trumpet, I went behind his back and made a good deal with the owner. Having satisfied the vendor I phoned the solicitor and said he should put my new offer in without delay. He thought he knew better and let the vendor stew for a few days. By the time he came to get the offer in it was *too late*! Two other interested parties had materialized and now there was a closing date. The result was that someone else bought the place. The vendor said he wasn't prepared to deal with a solicitor like that. The solicitor in question explained that in Scotland solicitors see themselves as advisors and not agents that carry out instructions. So be firm, but let your solicitor negotiate if you think it necessary. It's a good idea to haggle a bit but stick to your guns when you *know* you're right, otherwise go to another solicitor. They charge enough and they're working for *you*, not the other way round. (So saying, we now have a wonderful solicitor who's businesslike and doesn't have an ego-axe to grind!)

Buying in England can be just as frustrating, of course—a sort of 'free for all' scramble if the economy and market is very volatile as it was in the Thatcherite years. We had tried buying in the Lake District in the late 'eighties but there was so much gazumping. Honestly, the price of a place we were putting an offer on went up by £10,000 a day. You're almost back to the 'Scarborough syndrome' again!

So, careful consideration as to what you want and where you want it has to be weighed against the place currently under review. Is it *really* suitable for your needs? It's so easy to get carried away with enthusiasm for something totally unsuitable, or to jump the gun—as we did, perhaps, in one desperate attempt to settle down and *get going*. (Fortunately we were able to make the property we bought work for us—though if we'd been more patient we *might* have found something more suitable and more profitable from day one.) Keep the following in mind:

Things to avoid!

1. A place that's really run down will cost you a lot of money and be hard work. (Of course, if you have the time and the money, as well as the inclination to get your hands dirty, refurbishing it can be very rewarding.)

2. Try to avoid an establishment that has no off-street parking, or a car park that's too small!

Maybe it's just the guests we attract, but quite a number of them are paranoid about the size of our car park. I suppose it's the crime today and people have a right to be worried. But we live in a backwater and nothing ever happens here, so when guests become neurotic about their cars we just stand back open-mouthed. But certainly, our car park *is* small. We have six rooms and six car spaces. If each person parks considerately (and most people do), there's room for everyone. But some people just come in and abandon their cars as if they were the only people staying so nobody else can get it. Even when we've politely asked them to re-align their car, they seem to forget or ignore our request! (Perhaps we're too polite and not forceful enough.) On one occasion a German guest more or less abandoned his minibus so that the next car (a Ford Escort) couldn't quite pull in off the pavement (about three inches of the tail remained sticking out of the gate). The owner of the Escort cancelled his second night's booking as a result and threatened legal action if his car was in any way damaged. He was so anxious and belligerent that my husband felt obliged to stand guard over his car *all night* (it was a cold night in October). We end up feeling guilty—but most guests are good drivers and cope beautifully. In fact, some are amazing and more often than not I have the impulsive desire to hug and kiss them.

Actually, maybe it's best to have no car park—for then there's no car park to complain about! This is not uncommon and I've worked in a few expensive hotels where the car park fills up quickly and guests just have to park in the street. They never seemed to mind. Yet we had one old gent who parked his car beautifully, only to come to the door, exasperated and fuming, saying he couldn't possibly stay since the parking would worry him too much and off he went!

White lines painted on the tarmac to indicate parking spaces will, of course, alleviate the problem.

3. Avoid a place with too many floors—unless you have a lift. Ground floor is best. So many people think they are disabled. It's sad but you'll find a 50-year old puffing and panting up to the first floor and yet we have one old lady with leg calipers come back year after year to stay in an attic room on the second floor. I think she must be over sixty (one of those ageless people). It depends on the type of guest you attract—but if you're building a small hotel then put all the rooms on the ground floor. You'll certainly attract more customers, including the vast number of 40-year old geriatrics. Actually, if you are building a custom-built hotel, then you must make the rooms 'accessible' for disabled. A great idea. The Tourist Board do a leaflet on accommodation for disabled.

Steep steps are intimidating to those who haven't stairs at home. Not that you can avoid steep stairs if the place already has them, but at least make sure there is a stair rail for the faint-hearted.

4. Avoid an establishment with small rooms. The size of the rooms is quite important to some, especially our American visitors. They have the illusion that our old Victorian buildings are like the Tardis—old and quaint on the outside, huge, glass, plastic and chrome on the inside. Really, I think they're expecting to walk into the Holiday Inn. Why do they choose Old Victorian for character when what they really want is modern American? (One American visitor cancelled his booking when he saw the average size of his double room, nevertheless asking us to hold the room while he tried to find another at a different establishment—even though it was already six in the evening and the busiest night of the season!) A good rule is certainly the bigger the better. Having said that, most of our guests are happy with our rooms where you could swing a cat but not an Irish Wolfhound. Our attic rooms are quite small in that they have sloping ceilings. You either love them or hate them. We charge less because of this and are careful to warn guests in advance that the cheaper price is because of the smaller size!)

5. In avoiding small rooms, try to avoid a place that has only single rooms, or only double rooms, or only twin-bedded rooms. Once again, the bigger the room the better, for then it can be adaptable for *any* purpose—family room, double, twin or indeed single. If every room can be a family room (containing one double bed and at least one single bed), that's best since then you have total flexibility and adaptability. It can be a double, twin, single or even a family room! We have a lovely 'pull out' bed in one of our family rooms. It fits snugly under the single bed and has a proper mattress. It makes the room even more adaptable. Not a lot of people have three kids nowadays so on the whole you should get away with two singles for the kiddies. We get a lot of golfers and they're generally happy to go three to a room—provided each man has his own separate bed! (Men are funny

about sharing beds, aren't they? Women might, but men definitely won't! Once we were asked to squeeze in as many Welsh rugby-supporters as possible, regardless of whether they had single beds or had to share double beds. The lads won't mind, the person making the booking reassured us. But inadvertently, one of the men found he was sharing a bed with the coach driver. He wouldn't have it. "You see, I don't *know* him!" he wailed poignantly!)

We try to keep our family rooms till last since if you have a double free then the next caller will want a twin and vice versa. Funny the way it happens, but if you have the family room left it can be anything.

Continentals prefer twin beds on the whole. To add to flexibility you can buy *zip-beds,* of course—two singles that can be zipped together.

Just a quick mention. The time of year you move into the hotel will be an important factor. We moved in at the beginning of March. This was perfect for us since the hotel is, for the most, seasonal. We had no plans to do anything to the hotel, just to run it for the season and see what it needed. This meant we were straight into cashflow but in a nice slow manner giving us time to *train* before the rush came. Had we bought in November we'd have had a whole winter to go through with very little cashflow. It depends on your situation but it is very important. If you see just what you want in December then try and put off the awful moment for a couple of months—i.e. persuade the vendors to go for a completion date suitable to you.

*   *   *

As a general rule, try to see things through potential guests' eyes. Ask yourself if *you* would be happy to stay in a place like this!

Remember, whatever you buy you might get stuck with for an awfully long time. So even if you're considering it just as a *stepping-stone,* don't buy something you don't like from the start. You have to *like* the building and *like* the location and *like* the business. I know it's what you make of it in the end, but you'll be there twenty-four hours a day. Don't rush into something unless you really want it. There's always another hotel coming on the market tomorrow—it may be *just* the one you were looking for.

CHAPTER 3

Of Tourist Boards and Advertising!

I don't suppose there's a part of the country that's not covered by some Tourist Board or other. They seem to vary slightly but are, on the whole, the same.

In our case we're covered by the Scottish Tourist Board. It's an organization we affectionately call the Mafia. We may at times feel we could do without it but now that it's so well entrenched into the hospitality industry and because so many of our prospective guests automatically seek their accommodation requirements through the Tourist Board, we can't afford *not* to belong (unless, I suppose, we were the owners of a super-duper five-star country-type hotel). We advertise with the Tourist Board and, to give it its due, we get most of our business through it.

Our first use of the Tourist Board is through the TIC (Tourist Information Center). We're lucky enough to have one of the best in Scotland and it's just across the river and green from us—so it's easy for the TIC staff to point us out to prospective guests. (Again, the importance of location comes to mind. Of course, if your hotel is off the beaten path and difficult to find, then being a member of the Tourist Board becomes virtually essential.)

You have to 'belong' or be a member of the local branch of the Tourist Board (in our case the Scottish Borders Tourist Board) in order to get business from the TIC. This costs us about £150 a year for B & B and hotel status and grading. For this you get your photo up on their wall and a page in their local visitors book. When visitors come and want to book a room through them the office staff give them a folder to look at and the visitor chooses whichever place he fancies. (The folder will contain photographs of and relevant information about your establishment.) The TIC then phones you to ask if you have the room the visitor wants. If you have they book it, give you the name and time of arrival of the guest and check the price. They give the visitor a piece of paper with the charges on. The visitor gives them 10% of your total cost which you have to reimburse. If the guest's bill is for £40, then you'd simply present him or her with a bill for £36. The TIC keeps the £4 for themselves as commission.

Nowadays, in order to be in the Tourist Board guides, your hotel or guesthouse (or B&B) has to be 'graded.' This means a Tourist Board Grading Officer will come to your hotel, go through it with you, give you advice (sometimes it can be very helpful) and tell you what you need to do to qualify for whatever grading you want to achieve. Every other year the Grading Officer comes incognito and spends the night, having dinner if you give meals and generally 'testing you out'—only to reveal himself (usually herself!) next morning after breakfast. He then goes through the same routine as the ordinary visit, but in more detail since he's had a whole evening in which to snoop—i.e. pull the bed out to make sure you've hoovered there, tasted your yummy breakfast and even questioned the other guests. One of our Officers was having a great time in the lounge after dinner with the other guests (she wondered if the atmosphere was always quite so convivial) and told them who she was. One of the guests promptly came to my private door and whispered in my ear that we had a spy in the house! (This same Officer once sneaked out of a B & B late one evening and drove home to do a pile of ironing that had been building up. She only lived in the next village!) In our first year we had no idea what to expect from the Grading Officer or who it would be—whether a couple or a single person, man or woman. We treated everyone with equal suspicion, especially single men! Quite early on in the season we had a single gentleman staying (we don't get a lot of singles); he seemed sort of *official* so we treated him with great deference and respect, trying to get just the right degree of friendliness. His supper was cooked to perfection, his wine cooled that extra bit in the freezer. We did everything bar lick his feet! Of course he *wasn't* the Grading Officer at all. (Strange to say we've never seen him again!)

Anyway, grades change from time to time, but at the moment are De Luxe, Highly Commended, Commended and Listed—and we now have a star system instead of crowns. These stars depend on quality rather than facilities and I think members of the public are going to be terribly confused. They were confused with the crown rating but there seems to be a lot of misunderstanding with the new stars. To know how to achieve your stars you should contact your local Tourist Board and get them to send you a leaflet on the subject since their criteria change such a lot. Needless to say the better the quality, the better the rating. We could go up in star rating if we spent a bit more on the place, but having a fantastic rating is not necessarily better for business.

De Luxe and Highly Commended attract more problem people than usual, since they often seem to create expectations far in excess of what the guest is likely to get for a small hotel or B & B. You'd think the price the guests are paying (usually under £20 per head) would be sufficient guide for them not to expect the Hilton! We get reports back from friends with high ratings and their guests are usually extra fussy with a host of attendant complaints: meals not cooked in the way they want, rooms too small, rooms too big. They often don't want to pay the price—yet they expect the quality. (In our own case we also find the more people pay the better they treat your place and the better they behave!)

Guests who seek out high gradings can be extra demanding. So if your ego won't allow you to go below De Luxe then be it on your own head! Remember, also, it could be embarrassing to slip back down to the lower grade if you changed your mind. One of my friends would love to go back from De Luxe to Highly Commended, but won't for fear of the humiliation such a downgrading might imply!

So why is 'Commended' preferable to 'Highly Commended'? Well, for one thing, people won't be intimidated by the higher grade and you'll attract more business. They may well choose your establishment with its 'Commended' grading as a place where they feel they can relax and put their feet up! (One guest actually took his socks off and literally put his feet up on the coffee table—I didn't mean *that* relaxed!) So a lower grade might actually be more relaxing for guests *and* owners. It's possible to achieve good quality without the paranoia and hassles that a higher grading may evoke with its expectation of excellence. And consider the cost of *maintaining* the higher grading. We were going to try for 'Highly Commended' after our first year but after the stories we heard we decided against it and would never change. This doesn't stop you having a superior quality place, of course—but you might want to reconsider if the Tourist Board suggests a 'Highly Commended' or 'De Luxe' grading. At the end of the day it's the most cost-effective grading that really counts—and the one that brings in the most profits.

Your best bet is to get a grading booklet from your local Tourist Office. Without it it's easy to fall short of the criteria required for a Tourist Board grading. You may think that just one bedside table for a double bed is sufficient. But you'll need one for *each* person in the bed plus a lamp. Two ashtrays, two comfortable chairs, luggage rack, normal sized wash basin, beds of good quality, full length mirror, dressing table with mirror, so many square meters per person, 100 watt bulb in the overhead light. Criteria vary from time to time so get a booklet and tick off each item as you get it in relation to the grading you want to achieve.

If you want to ingratiate yourself and quite possibly learn something, especially if you've never done this sort of thing before, then enroll for a one-day course like 'Welcome Host.' (The Tourist Board frequently offers one-day or two-day courses, usually geared to marketing.) In the 'Welcome Host' course offered by the Scottish Borders Tourist Board they show you how to deal with customers in all situations, how to keep them happy, what little extras you can provide to make them eager to come back for more. I think it's a bit of a hoot but really, if you've never done it before, then it's probably worthwhile. (You get a special icon or emblem you can display in your advertising, not to mention a badge to display proudly on your jumper!)

The Scottish Borders Tourist Board actually offers lots of little courses. There's a new one that is a step up from 'Welcome Host,' called 'Scotland's Best.' There are also half-day courses and day courses in the off-season—computing, languages (conversational relating to hotels), and first-aid which is a good idea. They love doing little things like this so ask them what's on this winter.

They do get a bit carried away sometimes—especially in the expectations of guests' needs. Here's a sample from a leaflet that tells the hotelier or guesthouse owner (or 'B & B' owner—whoever is crazy enough to join the scheme) what to do for guests on a walking holiday:

A separate space should be made available for drying outdoor clothing and footwear at an ambient temperature of approx. 30 deg C; two options of design: it is possible to use a heater to warm the room to a temperature that causes evaporation of water in the clothing…heat source should not be a naked flame but be a convector or fan heater or radiator (outdoor clothes are easily damaged). There will sometimes be a considerable amount of water vapor produced during drying and extractor fans or ventilation holes in the ceiling or near at the top of the walls will help air flow dissipate this vapor. The additional cost of this system is high…a much more cost effective method is to install dehumidifiers…the room should be fairly well sealed with vents or extractor fans (NB the door should not have a lock); a small heater can be installed to help bring the temperature up initially but will have to be on permanently. Dehumidifiers will cost approx. £650…a structure for hanging clothing up around the heat source…should be fitted to the walls of the drying rooms that allows both clothing and boots to be elevated above the ground…

There's a whole page of this. You should be able to offer packed lunches and provide flasks (fair enough!). There's a *whole page* devoted to what should and should not be in a packed lunch. You should be able to offer late evening meals and early breakfasts from 7 a.m., hot drinks on arrival, not to mention weather forecasts! This is for serious walkers and accommodation providers who seriously want to take in walkers. I suppose if you have time on your hands, then it must be wonderful to be so attentive to minute details—and remember, you're doing it for a sum that's probably under £20 per head for bed and breakfast! Your life would need to be devoid of anything else! I suppose if you have a place in the Highlands that has no prospect of trade apart from walkers, then this is your lot in life (apart from wonderful scenery, of course).

To be fair to the Tourist Board, though, they probably have a more indepth concept of walkers and their requirements than we do—though it's possible that in pandering to their needs they have created peripatetic Frankenstein monsters! We always thought of walkers as open-minded, wonderful people—salt of the earth and all that. After all, they love being in the open air and are presumably reasonably energetic and capable of coping with trivial problems. In fact, my husband Charles and I are fond of walking ourselves! But our experience of walkers has been far from favorable. They're much like our American guests—aggressive consumers who must have come out of a very pampered background, not the jolly, breezy outdoorsy people we once knew. One woman phoned to say she'd be walking to a point about three miles from us and could we pick her up? This is not unusual in itself since we're expected to cart their luggage round for them anyway; but on asking this woman what time she would arrive she said, "Oh, anything between 3pm and 7pm". "And you want me to wait for you, is that correct?" I asked with disbelief. "Yes," she replied casually, as though she normally had hotel owners (who have absolutely nothing else to do) waiting two or three hours for her to turn up. I think the service industry is possibly the only industry where you really see the downside of people. Don't get me wrong—we meet a lot of wonderful people too. It's just that it's the daft ones that stick in the memory!

The first thing you need to ask yourself before you start to advertise your place is *who* do you want in your home/hotel? What is your target group? Well, what sort of people come to your area? If you have a place overlooking Blackpool pier then you're not going to want to advertise in *Horse & Hound* or *Vogue*. You may have a particular market in mind but just check that these sort of people would actually *want* to come to the area you're in. If you're in a city then fell walkers are not likely to visit you. What sort of guides are they likely to buy? What sort of newspapers will they read? Are they young and not wanting to pay too much or are they middle aged and expect a bit more quality, having more to spend? (For instance, most of our middle-aged and older guests insist on *en-suite* facilities.) What are you going to charge them? Too little can be as off-putting as too much. Seeing things, for the moment, from the consumers' point of view, I reckon you get what you pay for (on the whole); I personally would never stay anywhere too cheap for fear that it's just not my type of place (I like a bit of comfort in my dotage!).

Once your business is up and running, or if it's a going concern, you'll find you're *inundated* with people wanting you to advertise with them. NEVER place an advert over the phone when you receive an unsolicited phone-call. There are many rogues out there and they can put a lot of pressure on you. Don't be frightened to tell them where to get off if they get stroppy. Just put the phone down. Don't attempt to argue the point—they'll always have an answer, even if you say you're 100% full all the time! The best thing is to say that you never advertise in a journal you have never seen. Ask for a copy to be sent to you with the advertising rates and tell them you'll get back to them. If they do send you a copy then they *are* bona fide—though it still doesn't mean their journal meets your needs. But at least it lets them know you're not going to be taken for a ride. Most of the people I ask to send me copies of their journal/papers never send me anything. There are lots of cowboys who don't even own a *typewriter*, let alone a publishing company! One of their lines is to phone to say they're just checking the wording of the advert you placed. If they read it to you and you agree it's okay then you're basically giving them permission to go ahead. (Another favorite ruse of theirs is to ask you what color you prefer your ad to be highlighted in. Charles—that's my husband, remember?—fell for this in our first year and plumbed for red, imagining it was for an ad that I must have placed without consulting him. The result? We were obliged to pay £100 for an ad in an esoteric publication that brought us *absolutely no business at all*!) The best way around this problem is to have just *one* person who is responsible for placing the advertising. Two or more can make the decisions, but if only one person deals with the actual journals, then he or she will know exactly what has been placed and where.

While I'm on the subject of rogues I'll just mention this—be careful of Faxes! Some rogues have recently been faxing hotels, requesting them to send them menus and brochures by return Fax. The number given is a continental number and it's one of those lines that costs a fortune and, of course, they make money from the Faxes received—obviously, at your expense. So beware!

Back to the subject in hand. One advertiser phoned to say my husband had already agreed to place an ad with her. I knew this wasn't true since I'm the only one who places the ads. She told me my husband must be stupid! (Well, he *can* be, but in this instance I gave him the benefit of the doubt.) I took her name and phoned her employers. Amazingly enough the agency was bona fide. I used to ask for the name and address of the caller before I'd let him or her speak to me. Some refused to give it to me with the most amazing reasons for not doing so. (They would say they're in the process of moving offices, that they're not allowed to give addresses and even "I'm new here, I don't know!") If they become obnoxious you can always threaten them with the DTI. If you're able to say no easily then you won't have a problem. It took me awhile to learn that I don't have to stand listening to hours of boring sales talk and that I can cut in and say no thank you. (Now, when Charles answers the phone and the caller asks to speak to the Manager or the 'person responsible for advertising,' he always hands the phone to me. Apart from his decision that I was to be the sole person responsible for placing the ads, it was mutually decided that I was the one with more sales resistance!)

There are a few holiday package firms about. We tried one called *Country Rovers/Scottish Roamin' Holidays* which used a voucher system for payment. In principle it was a good idea and since we didn't get our full price for the vouchers the scheme allowed us to charge the guest a pre-agreed fixed supplement for *en-suite* facilities. But a lot of people didn't want to pay the supplement since they had already paid a fortune for the vouchers at home. One man (a huge German) refused to pay the supplement, saying he hadn't *asked* for an *en-suite* room. (We only *have* en-suite rooms, a fact which was clear enough in his guide book.) I offered to call the police to sort it out and he paid up ungraciously. One Dutch lady had a novel reason for not paying the *en-suite* supplement. We had given her our best family room and she was delighted when she saw the room. Yet when she came down to pay in the morning she refused to pay the supplement on the grounds that the room didn't have a private *sitting room* attached to the bedroom!

We took on the cheaper voucher scheme on the understanding that it was meant as a last-minute top-up, like a standby booking normally made on the day before the room is required. Guests would normally phone on the day or the night before to book. But in practice many of these bookings were made well in advance, even months before, which meant they blocked the better and more expensive mid-season bookings. The scheme also required us, as the hoteliers, to book their next night's accommodation for them—an ordeal which often took ages! (Usually we had to do this in the middle of serving the evening meal!) You might have had to phone twenty hotels before you got satisfaction. If this happens in the middle of breakfast (or the evening meal) and the guest's English is limited, it can be a somewhat exasperating experience. Communication was of course part of the problem. The guests were supposed to *say* they were from the agency when they booked. That way we could put them in our smaller rooms on the second floor since they weren't paying much. They often didn't say anything till they came to pay in the morning. We had a paranoid old Canadian woman with her poor tortured husband in our best family room for a week and didn't know they were voucher people till the day before they left—when her husband presented me with the vouchers. We had lost quite a lot of money so I felt obliged to charge them a bit extra for the *en-suite* facilities since they were supposed to tell me they were 'Roamers.' The woman was *not* amused. She was so angry in fact that she wouldn't talk to us when we served her breakfast. She had been a thoroughly neurotic person and had the whole town running around doing her bidding. We were pleased to see her go, not just because she had stopped speaking to us. (Actually, it was something of a relief when she stopped talking since it gave us time to get on with our work!) I felt a bit guilty since her long-suffering husband had been penalized too. Anyway, would you believe it, a year later a call came from Canada. "Hello, is that Jo? Can you guess who this is?" Quite frankly I hardly dared to guess. It *couldn't* be. Yes, it *was*. She wanted to come back but not on that 'horrid voucher scheme.' She would pay, she said. 'like normal people!' She came, she terrorized the whole town yet again and left us all quite exhausted with her frenetic activity. However, she left with a smile on her face—and our kids £40 better off in tips! So you never can tell what kind of treatment will please a demanding guest. Or what repercussions a voucher-system might have!

Speaking of demanding guests—I'm reminded of another guest at an hotel I once worked for (500 bedrooms). We had an old lady staying who was very eccentric. One of the young trainee managers escorted her to her room on her first visit. He made a chance remark after she had said the bed was too high—to the effect that 'it was worth it when you got up there!' His reply so impressed her that thereafter she insisted this same under manager escort her to her room *every* night after dinner. I wonder if he ever got a day off? She used to swan down the huge spiral staircase in the evening looking like a smaller version of Barbara Cartland, fully locked into evening gown and tiara.

But I digress! The voucher schemes *can* work. We passed the idea on to a few friends who have been very grateful since it satisfies *their* price market and they don't have to collect supplements since they don't have *en-suite* facilities. (In their case, they simply take the bookings, collect the vouchers from the guests when they leave, send the vouchers to the company—and in a week or two they receive a cheque for the voucher amounts.) You'll find the address of the scheme at the back of the book. The system may have changed, so do read the small print before you use the scheme.

We had quite good use of a voucher company recently. They phoned to say they want to use us again the following year but would we allocate them 'x' number of rooms on a permanent basis through the season? They'll cancel the arrangement, say, two weeks before if they don't fill the rooms. This is no good to us. In the season we fill up anyway on account of our existing advertising with the Scottish Tourist Board and AA. Your position might be similar, so please be careful if you're asked to allocate rooms to a firm. I gave this firm 5% which is my usual agents' commission.

In our neck of the woods the Scottish Borders Tourist Board run a scheme which is actually an *excellent* one for the locale. It's a package golfing holiday called *The Freedom of the Fairways*. We've done very nicely out of it and got a lot of repeat trade. We quote a price, whatever we want, plus the price of the golf ticket and advertise it as a package. Because golf is so expensive in other regions (especially in the south of England) people think it's incredibly cheap here. We do our own advertising in golfing magazines or golfing newspapers since this method has proved much more effective than the advertising the Tourist Board does on our behalf. (In the Scottish Borders Tourist Board's 'Freedom of the Fairways' leaflet your establishment has to compete with all the others who are also members of the Freedom of the Fairways scheme). Eighteen golf clubs in the district are in the scheme. The guest gets two tickets per day for either three or five days which entitles him to play on any of these eighteen courses. As I said, there are golf magazines and golfing papers. The latter are cheaper to advertise with but it's worth giving both a try if you can get a deal going with a few local courses.

The Tourist Board do fishing and walking schemes too, but we don't belong to those. We do get the odd hunter. They get up at about 3 a.m. and come back midday for breakfast. It's a bit of a bother but I can see the reason in this so I put up with it. Not that is happens very often.

Anyway, you can always look out for schemes of your own. Do you want to make a deal with a local restaurant, say, to do dinner dances? Agree to advertise *together*. You provide, say, two nights B & B plus one dinner, on the understanding that the second night the guests go to the local restaurant for a dinner dance—at an all-inclusive price. We did a bit of this, especially three-night breaks that included a dinner-dance on New Year's Eve and Valentine's Day, where the restaurant provided the dinner-dance. There are lots of things you can do. Perhaps you live near an old steam railway and could do a deal with rail tickets, then advertise in the railway mags? What about cyclists if you're on a popular cycling route, or even horse riding, go-karting, or activity holidays to be held locally? See what's going on in your area and cash in on it. If you can't offer a *meal deal* then you could offer three days for the price of two. Your library will have books on special interests. You could browse through the many different activity magazines in Smiths for ideas. Are you an ex-teacher of languages? You could do language weekends for adults wishing to brush up on their skills. Or, in the off-season, present writing weekends where an established writer (or writers) will present a course of talks with helpful advice.

So where do I advertise?

Once you've discovered who your guests are going to be then you'll have honed down where to advertise. There are quite a few little local type publications such as *The Dalesman* or *The Scots Magazine*. It also depends on what type of holiday you're offering, of course. We advertise in a Glasgow paper (*The Sunday Post*) for our spring and autumn short breaks since Glasgow is a comfortable car ride away, not too far if people are coming for just a couple of days. We chose a Sunday paper because people have more time to read it and because it has a longer shelf life than a daily paper. We've tried the holiday supplements that fall out of Sunday newspapers, but they seem less effective.

Really, we've found that advertising in the main books is the best (having tried everything else). The AA gets us quite a bit of business. We tried the RAC and they put the wrong photo in, gave us a free ride the next year (though we never actually saw the publication) and we didn't get a single person from it. Curtains for them. The AA have inspectors that call once a year. It's a good thing since it keeps us on our toes. It's easy to let things slip. They're exceptionally nice people and come and go in about an hour. You can even ask their advice! They give a 'Q' rating for quality. I don't think facilities count so much with them since it would be in the advertising anyway. They do have a 'Selected' rating and a 'Premier Selected.' This means you're the *bees knees* and I think the ad is almost free for being such a goody goody. Advertising with the AA is expensive, since you have to pay for the ad costs plus membership costs plus inspection fees, *plus* the cost of a color photo if you want one. (The same series of costs are also true, of course, in the case of Tourist Board.) Once again, you'll find the AA address in the back of the book. Remember to ask for a rate card.

The only other large holiday guidebooks we use are those published by the Tourist Board. That's also expensive. In fact, belonging to them can be *very* expensive—but on the whole it *works*. We have a color photo in the *Hotel and Guest House Guide* which bumps up the price—but I'm sure its worth it. Try to get your ad on the top right-hand page. Apart from advertising in the *Hotel and Guest House Guide* as well as the *B & B Guide* published by the Scottish Tourist Board, we also advertise in their local Scottish Borders Tourist Board 'Where to Stay' booklet. This contains a myriad of local B & B's, guesthouses and hotels. This isn't as expensive as the books and we do get business from it, so we keep it going. I sometimes wonder, because these books have a long shelf life, whether one wouldn't get away with advertising every *other* year—but I haven't been brave enough to try it! Our advertising comes to about £3,000 a year. In April we're usually 90% full. May is much the same. Thereafter we'll be 99.9% full till the end of September/October. No pain, no gain!

There are a few very good guidebooks which are still popular but you can't go in them all. Your best bet is really to pop along to W.H.Smiths and have a good look in their guidebooks and see which you fancy. After all, most of your customers will get their guidebooks from them too! Don't advertise in something that's not widely available.

And don't forget, your **HOTEL** or *B & B* sign will attract custom, or detract if it looks a mess. Another good idea is to use a floodlight. We have a floodlight that lights up a large sign that says **HOTEL** (clearly visible from the main A68 route), *and* another that lights up the front of the building. This has attracted guests well into the night! (Once all the rooms are let, of course, we switch off the floodlights!)

Writing a successful advertisement

It's a good idea to get a copy of a good guide—one that you would probably use for *your* hotel. Have a good look through it and see what your competitors do. It will give you an idea of the local pricing if you want to be competitive. See whether they accept credit cards, cheques, give dinners, take dogs, allow smokers, have *en-suite* facilities, central heating and a whole host of other things. You'll then soon see which are the best ads as well as have a good look at the competition.

You'll need to mention all the relevant things which most people need to know without giving them information diarrhea. I would mention at least the following if going in a guide book:

- Whether or not you're in the countryside and how far you're away, by foot or by car, from local amenities, pubs and shops.

- Your location, if possible with a map. Try to give directions on how to find your establishment—e.g. 'last right when going south off A7 as you leave town.' You won't have a lot of room so make it brief. At least this way people will find you. (Guests have sometimes said that *knowing* how to find us was the reason for choosing us.)

- *Say* if you are all *en-suite*. This means a lot to a lot of people.

- If you have televisions in rooms as well as hospitality trays, mention it.

- What meals you provide (if any) and a price guide.

- Your room (or B & B) tariff. This will normally go at the bottom of the ad.

- If you take credit cards. Put the little **VISA** and **MASTERCARD** logos on the ad, down the side, say, to make it more eye-catching.

- Parking, if you have it—but if it's limited, use the word *limited* to avoid the possibility of eyeball-to-eyeball arguments! As I mentioned earlier, my husband stayed up all one night to guard a guest's car since our brochure said we had parking and his car was sticking out about 3" into the pavement—thanks to somebody else's bad parking. (I've yet to order two tons of pig poo to be delivered to that guest's front door!)

- The guide books don't allow you much room for your copy so make the most of it. If you have anything that really *is* a perk like a pool, or generous parking, then get it in!

- If you don't want smokers, then this is the time to mention it since otherwise your ad will certainly attract droves of smokers. We take them though we really don't like it—and it seems so unfair to the next guest who may be a non-smoker. But from our experience the majority of our guests smoke. (Of course, a non-smoking policy may well attract a good many non-smoking guests—so may well pay dividends.)

The grading officer from the Tourist Board (or AA) will generally help you do your write-up but do have a look at what other people are saying. You need to say what you really feel is *You* (such as 'clean, modern bungalow / large Victorian villa').

Here's a few I've just taken out of one of the guide books:

- *A charming family-run hotel just off A66 to/from Carlisle. Situated beside river, it enjoys panoramic views of the castle and town. Five minutes walk from shops, restaurants and pubs. All rooms en-suite with color TV. CH. Choice of menu, wines and snacks. Price from £25 B & B.*

- *A very secluded farmhouse at the end of a long lane to the south of Kendal providing friendly service and comfortable accommodation. There is a cozy lounge...bedrooms, while not en-suite, have private bathrooms and shower rooms.*

Always mention Location:

- *Immaculately maintained, this modern detached private house is* set *in a quiet estate...*

- *Situated in a quiet road close to town center and amenities, this family owned guesthouse offers pleasant bedrooms...*

The name of the hotel and address is at the top of the ad with the phone number. Always check the phone number in the proofs, with the star rating from the Tourist Board and credit card logos down the side.

For our short break ads in the Sunday paper (not a national) we chose classified since we are charging very little for the package and didn't want to spend much advertising (cost about £50 per insertion; there's a special rate—three insertions for the price of two—which has proved to be worthwhile. After three insertions the ad will draw very few people; most will respond after the first insertion). The people we were trying to attract were more likely to look through the classified. We made it as brief as possible. Here's a typical sample:

BORDERS.—A charming family run hotel overlooking Dedburgh abbey. All rooms en-suite with col TV, res lic, STB 3 crown Comm. 3 nights DBB, only £66! (this was a few years ago). *Tel (01809) 501338.*

(Try to start your ad with an 'A' or a 'B' since then your ad will come almost first, being alphabetically listed. In our case we're usually near the top since we use the header: **BORDERS**.)

As I said, we get three for the price of two. On the whole we got quite a lot from the first, more from the second and very little from the third. We do this in the early part of the year (March, April) when most people stay tucked up indoors, and then late like November. It's hard work (dangerously approaching the Scarborough syndrome!), since you're charging very little for the evening meal which is generally a set menu. Nevertheless, it's a very effective way of extending your season and making ends meet through a long hard winter!

Display ads cost a lot more but it does depend on who you're trying to attract and what you expect them to pay. We had display ads in golf magazines which did no better than the little classified we'd put in before. If an ad stops working then stop doing it. Try again later if you like. Some people cut ads out and keep them for a year or more (I do!).

We use display ads in the big guides plus the small line entries.

We also find a photograph helps, not a sketch. Remember the days when people went off to Majorca to find the hotel wasn't even built, in spite of a very convincing and fetching sketch of the hotel? People like to *see* what they're getting. (We have line drawings on our brochure since these are cheaper to reproduce; but we compensate with a stick-on photograph of the hotel, mass-produced in advance by a photographic service. See the next heading!)

Brochures

There are many different types of brochure and it's really a question of how much you're prepared to pay. The local B & B's seem to prefer a card type which folds out and has a photo on the outside. You can have up to four small photos on the front or just one. On the inside is information about your hotel (plus a map) with room for your tariff. Don't have the tariff printed but leave it blank so you can alter it when you choose. Just write it in by hand as you send them out. These brochures are quite small, 5" x 2 1/2," but you can vary size and content. You can in fact get anything you want. You could have a card with photo and bare facts which will never change, then an insert for things which will alter from year to year with prices of dinners, tariffs, etc. on cheaper paper. Go for the best you can afford. (Presentation is always important: your brochure may be the first impression you give to a potential guest.) There are addresses of people who do brochures in the back, but your local printer can do it too.

We actually got our latest one done by our local printer. Our daughter did a sketch of the building which we had put on the front; she also did a sketch of the dining room with a view through the window of the Abbey.

An artistic guest from Germany did a rather nice sketch of golfers holed in by sheep, so we got his permission to use it in the brochure and we gave him the credit under his sketch which looks friendly—suggesting an informal friendly relationship between ourselves and our guests! Because there is only a sketch on the front and we know how important photos are, we use a superb firm in Hull (address in back) which prints any photos to various sizes. These are on adhesive paper, so all you have to do is peel them off and stick them on the front of your brochure or wherever you want them. If you have a stupendous view from your bedrooms, you could do a photo of that too—whatever comes to mind. On the back we have our name and address and phone number and a map.

The brochure is simplicity itself, which helps to keep down the cost and is easily reproduced by our local print shop. (We can even reproduce it on our IBM computer, with the help of a scanner.) It's just a nice A4 colored piece of shiny paper that folds into three. Have the printers fold them for you. On the front we stick our photo and the Tourist Board stickers with our star rating. You can buy these cheaply from the Tourist Board after your grading has been confirmed. It brightens up the brochure.

When people write and confirm their booking to us, Charles always confirms back, saying we are looking forward to their visit and encloses a copy of our brochure.

Quite a few people will ask for your card. This could be another opportunity to give them a copy of your brochure, though it would be cheaper to give them a calling card for them to take away with them. You could also leave cards (or your brochures) at local petrol stations or restaurants, pubs, castles, or shops, as an extra form of marketing. Many of our last-minute guests arriving late will have picked up one of our cards at the local petrol station.

When guests arrive one has to ask them to register. This is required by law, yet it's another area where you can do some marketing research. We don't use a book, partly because people feel obliged to write how wonderful you are, and the next person feels obliged to do the same and its nauseating. Guests are actually supposed to fill in the book as they arrive, so how are they supposed to know how wonderful you are before they've even stayed? We had one guest refuse to register in the book. He said *anyone* could come along and look at his address, phone his criminal friends and have the house burgled while he's away. Good point! It was a wonderful excuse to get rid of said crass book. I immediately had registration slips made. All you need is the name and address, passport number if your guests are foreign, and car number—in case they do a bunk, I suppose! (Not once in ten years has that happened to us, touch wood!) The main advantage of registration slips, however, is that it enables you to include a space where you can ask the guest where he or she found out about your hotel. In this way you can keep an eye on which advertising is working.

My daughter did a lovely painting of the hotel and we had postcards made of it. They went down very well but we eventually ran out and haven't had any more done. People loved them. Get someone from the local Grammar or Poly; they'll be pleased to earn a few quid doing a nice painting or line drawing of your place. Give them the credit. It could go in their portfolio. You could even sell the cards to the guests.

Letterheads

We've always used very simple letterheads which a lot of private hotels use from Able Label (address in back). They give you a choice of typescript and color of paper. Its very cheap, especially compared with professional printing. It really depends on what sort of hotel you're running. Quite frankly, six bedrooms at our level doesn't warrant anything posh—it might smack of overkill and result in false expectations. We do have a letterhead on the computer which we use for special occasions. We just have the name of the hotel, address, phone number and our names. We find that half A4 (in other words, A5) is large enough. This really is a matter of personal choice. Nevertheless, you have to bear in mind that your letter (with the letterhead and quality of paper) is often the first impression you're making on a prospective guest.

If we give out local brochures to guests in the post we put our own sticky address label on the back of the envelopes. These are from Able Label (address in back) and are handy for all sorts of things.

Mail Shots

Not a fantastic idea if you're small! I did this with golfing (sending details of our Freedom of the Fairways scheme to golf clubs) and got very little response from it. You could send reminders to past guests that you're still alive but they'll probably come back to you anyway. Guests are very loyal and if treated well will come back time and again. One becomes so fond of some guests it's sad to see them leave and one feels guilty charging them.

You could mail-shot guests of the previous owners to say *you're* now running the hotel. Write an article about yourself if you have any special interests or about your hotel if it's at all unusual and send it to a suitable magazine as an article. Make sure your name and phone number(s) are mentioned. This is good free advertising. Write to clubs and ask to see their club newsletter. It might be worth advertising in and will cost less than national advertising.

Internet

This is becoming an acceptable way of advertising for booking ahead and if you have your own computer with modem then you can browse around and see who the best people are for advertising with. The AA do a nice display ad on your behalf and, of course, are well known. However, guests can't really take their computers with them on holiday so I'd say there's no rush yet! Nevertheless, this is a growth area and before long it may be to your advantage to have your own website on the Internet. In a panel discussion on *Sky TV's Computer Channel* (29-12-1997) it was claimed that a remote B&B in Tenby in South Wales had increased its trade by leaps and bounds by having its own website advertisement. Since then it has become almost imperative for a hotel or guesthouse to have a web presence. It is also undeniable that this is a cheaper form of advertising than the traditional printed media via the tourist boards and the AA and, indeed, many hotel and guesthouse owners are now turning to the Internet as their major marketing outlet.

A hotel and guesthouse register, or guide, that has grown phenomenally, and which is certainly worth advertising with, is found at the Internet site *www.travelaccommodation.co.uk*, and can be contacted by email at *hotel@travelaccommodation.co.uk*.

*   *   *

You can speak to ten different people about where they advertise and you'll probably get ten different answers. Isn't that helpful! We know that where we advertise works for *us*. The chances are they'll work for you too. We're not very adventurous when it comes to advertising but then we're as full as we want to be. I would recommend you try the main books first, if you can afford their hellish rates. If you're on a main road with hundreds of cars passing each day, then maybe you don't need to advertise very much. I've only come across one hotelier so far who says he doesn't advertise. He runs a hotel up north which is basically on a golf course and relies almost solely on repeat trade. Lucky him! Actually, that's something to aim for, isn't it? 100% repeat trade or referrals!

CHAPTER 4

All that luvelly lolly!
So what can I charge?

The price you set, or the tariff, depends on your market. See what your competitors are charging and go with the flow! You can alter your tariff at a later date if you want. One thing to keep in mind, though—you must have your prices written down and displayed in a public place in your hotel. The authorities will check, so don't forget to do this.

Naturally you'll charge according to quality and facilities. For instance, if you have *en-suite* bedrooms, a small bar and give dinner, all of good standard, then you'll be entitled to charge more than the little B & B up the road. If you're taking over from someone else, then you'll have a guideline from them. Don't make any radical changes at first. Watch the guidebooks and phone around and snoop. People do it to me. I can tell when I'm being 'snooped' at!

No doubt you'll have a 'high season' and a 'low season.' Some places charge the same throughout the year, especially if they have only businessmen. However, the chances are you're seasonal, like us. We charge a few pounds more per head in the high season which for us is June to end of September. Our rooms on the second floor carry the same tariff all year round: they're attic rooms, smaller with sloping ceilings, so we couldn't charge too much for them anyway. By keeping their tariff down we're making them more marketable.

We're considering keeping to the same tariff all year round, for when people come in the winter and get a reduction it actually costs a lot more to keep them—especially when you take the heating costs into account. Furthermore, winter—in a way—is our time off. The question is: do we really *want* to encourage winter trade? (Or to rephrase it, are we desperate enough to trade through the winter! However, by keeping the tariff lower in the winter, we're making the rooms more marketable in the off-season.)

However, apart from minor variations in room tariffs, try not to have guests in different price ranges. In other words, don't mix your market—neither group of guests will like it. Adopt the same quality and target-group throughout the hotel. A middle-aged, conservative group of people will not want to share the dining room with a group of boisterous young folk, or workmen engaged in the construction of the nearby petrol station. When all is said and done, people are more snobbish and class conscious than they care to admit! So it's not a good policy to fill your rooms at any cost!

How do guests pay? Well, you have three options:

Cash

If you're planning to own a small B & B then most people will probably pay you in cash. That's very straightforward. Put it in the bank quickly before you spend it! It's like sand—or water—that runs all too easily through your fingers

Cheques *(or checks in Americanese!)*

Some B & B's refuse cheques. A lot of people use cheques and you don't really pay any more to put a cheque in the bank as you do cash. My bank charges 20p for each cheque deposited. Remember to get the cheque card number on the back of the cheque. I never used to, but got caught out once. I wrote to the person whose cheque bounced, saying how disappointed I was since I trusted him—and he duly sent me a new cheque by return! Not a bad record after about 1500 cheques. Take their cheque card number, though. We're fortunate since we have just the sort of guests I feel I *can* trust. (If I feel 'iffy' about someone I take his or her bank-guarantee-card number.)

Credit Cards

We accept credit cards, but a lot of B & B's don't. We actually use this to our advantage in our advertising—by displaying the **VISA** and **MASTERCARD** logos. A friend has only just started to use this facility, since she found more and more of her guests were asking to pay by credit card. She doesn't advertise the fact, but she uses them if guests ask. Many B & B or Guest House owners are reluctant to offer credit card facilities because of the 5% or so commission the credit-card company charges the retailer or accommodation provider. In our case we've found the cost well worth while because of the number of additional guests credit-card facilities attract—and, in any case, it's possible to negotiate a lower commission charge, especially if you're a member of a Tourist Board. Just ask your bank to send someone along from their credit-card office. They'll come and explain things and get you to sign a form.

They'll give you a small machine and a customer number. You just pay the credit card slips into the Bank and the money's yours (and the Tax man's!). It's really very simple. Once a month you'll get a summary telling you that they have debited your bank account with around 3% of your previous month's credit-card takings. You can shop around from bank to bank to see which gives the best rates—but they're all very similar. Credit cards don't bounce—apart from one I put through in error! I put the man's *cheque-guarantee* card through instead of his *credit card* (shows how incredibly observant I am!). Of course it came bouncing back like a rubber ball. I phoned the equally absent-minded gentleman to explain what an idiot I had been and he very kindly sent me a cheque.

One thing worth bearing in mind when you have the credit card facility is that you can take someone's card details as confirmation of a room. If they're making a booking for the same day they're due to arrive, say after six, then you're entitled to ask for their card number, name and expiry date. If they fail to turn up you could charge them for the lost room—that's if you have lost business as a result of holding the room. This forces people into a situation where they are obliged to let you know if they change their mind and decide not to come or if they're likely to arrive later than the time specified—otherwise you could charge them. Now here's an important piece of advice! When you join up with the card company, *be sure to ask for a Guarantee Hotel Reservations Agreement Form.* They won't tell you about this but if you don't have one signed, then the client can actually phone his/her card company and cancel the payment you have taken from them.

Some people put the cash back in their pocket when they see your credit card signs. It's up to you, but I'd say go for it. It's a form of advertising as well as an incentive, and some people most certainly will stay with you because of it.

Bills

Some people just use a receipt book—the sort of thing you can buy at Smiths. This is probably fine if you're small. I went a bit overboard at first and had some especially made which were self carbonating. This is much more expensive than ordinary printing. I thought I would need a copy for the accountant and it would be handy when I wrote the things the guests had had into my daily accounts sheet. However, I've found that I can work it without the extra expense of carbon! My bills look like this:

Rosebank Hotel

Abbeyview Road

Dedburgh

TD2 6NN

01809 501338

Accommodation . . . .

Dinner . . . .

Snacks . . . .

Bar . . . .

Misc . . . .

Total . . . .

If you just do B&B then this might be overkill. However, guests *do* like to have things itemized if they've had more than bed and breakfast. Your personal bill also means they have another copy of your phone number if they lose your brochure and they want to come again. If you have an E-mail address and your own web site, why not include the email and website URL too?

Some observations about paying guests!

Some people shop around to find the right price. Don't be offended. You might tell them it's £20 per head, and don't be surprised if they ask you if that's the room price or even if it includes dinner! They probably haven't stayed away from home for the past ten years. Sometimes they say they'll go and check with their spouses and you may not see them again. Some are not at all embarrassed to say they can't afford it. It's so much more pleasant if they're honest, especially if it's late and you feel you *could* let your last room for a bit less! Some come in and ask to see the room first. They make a big deal thumping the beds, checking the sheets, poking around in the bathroom (lifting the toilet seat and peering into the bowl!), looking out of the window, rearranging the tea tray, moving a chair. By this time you may as well leave them to it and tell them you'll be downstairs if they want you. What all this messing about usually means is they can't afford it but are too embarrassed to say so. If you really want them to stay, then tell them diplomatically that there's a less expensive alternative: "Ah, we do have a cheaper room. Perhaps you'd like to see it too?" Do you want to compromise? It depends on how busy you are and I suppose how awkward you feel at the moment. Some people insist on haggling, which I hate. (This applies especially to continentals from France and Italy.)

Two very old American ladies came in a few months ago. They asked for a twin room, not too expensive, on the ground floor with a bathroom and hard beds. We don't have ground-floor rooms but they allowed me to show them one of the family rooms which have lovely beds (we gets lots of compliments about them). It was hard to suppress a giggle as these two old and very heavily made-up ladies bounced up and down on each bed in turn. Lifting the duvet covers and checking the sheets, they asked: "Is it warm?" "Well, how long is a piece of string?" said I, tongue in cheek as I closed the window. (Being well into the spring, it wasn't at all cold.) I pointed out the two radiators and the electric fire which they promptly put on. They did the usual survey of the room, inspecting the bathroom with minute attention. I had to explain how the shower worked to each one *ad nausea* and set it at just the right spot. I then had to explain how the electric kettle worked and tell them no, they didn't have to boil water for the 'sink' (do they have Star Trek 'replicators' at home!). Having satisfied themselves it was okay they wanted to 'do a deal.' I was beginning to wish they'd go elsewhere, so to give them a discount to stay seemed rather a ridiculous move on my part. No, I couldn't offer a discount, I said politely. Well, they replied, what was the discount for their being old and batty? (That wasn't quite how they put it.) "Could we have a discount if we shared with another guest?" I was flabbergasted! Did they mean share a bedroom? I refrained from heavy irony and assumed they meant the bathroom. (I really don't think the couple in the next room would have been too pleased to have these dear old ladies tripping through their room at the dead of night to relieve themselves!) But I assumed they meant a cheaper room that wasn't *en suite*—which was not possible since all our rooms have their own bathrooms.

In the end they condescended to stay at the rate I originally quoted. I then spent the next 15 minutes describing how they could get to town in order to find a pub meal. It's really simple since town consists of the high street and that's it! One lady kept interrupting and the other put her right with a peremptory statement: "Look, Mavis, *I'm* doing the driving. Shut up and let the lady explain to *me!*" They duly signed in and went off in the direction of the pub. I said they couldn't get lost but they assured me they'd been lost many times since arriving in the UK. I think they must have escaped from an asylum.

Off they went in search of a bar for a stiff drink. I did the same. Would you believe it, two hours later they turned up and handed me the key. "The beds are, after all, a little too soft," they explained. I saw through them, of course, and replied icily: "You mean, you've been looking for something cheaper *all* this time!" I went upstairs, put the fire off, made the beds again and rearranged the room. They'd been like a circus act! But at least they weren't toffee-nosed—they just couldn't afford the room. (I suppose the previous two hours had been spent driving other landladies bananas and jumping on every bed in the district!)

Sometimes it's best not to have people who don't want to pay your price, otherwise *you'll* end up paying the price! Charles let an Israeli family in who managed to haggle and got our best family room for almost free for his family of four. By morning, apart from the mess, they had managed to rip the electric shower half off the wall. The moral is not to let people in who don't want to pay the price!

We have a 'dog show' weekend every June. Charles had a call from a woman wanting a family room for the Saturday night. He quoted our normal price, £21 per adult and half price for children and she said she'd think about it and rang off. A short while later I answered the phone to the same woman. She was obviously phoning around for the best price and didn't realize she had already rung our number. I'm an inquisitive person and when she asked for a family room price on 'Dog Saturday' I asked how many children she had (I needed to know how many and their ages in order to give her an accurate quote). "Oh," she replied breezily, "I don't have any children. The room is for me and my two Dobermans." I was surprised. "Isn't your husband coming? Is it just for you and your dogs?" I asked. "Yes, just me and the dogs." I asked if she wouldn't prefer a double or twin room (we have no single rooms), given that she was only one person. No, she wanted plenty of room for her dogs. No doubt she wanted a bed for them too, since some people *do* let their dogs sleep on the beds—even *in* the bed on one occasion, judging from the hairs on the sheets! I quoted as though it was her and her husband and a half-price child, seeing as she was insisting on a family room and for a time when there was great demand for our rooms. "Don't you think that's a bit mean?" she asked, drawing in her breath. "No," I explained. "The room is meant for families and that is a family price. You could have a twin at a twin price." "Thank you," she said icily, putting down the phone. Would you believe it, she called back *again*, thinking she would get Charles again who, she thought, had quoted £21 for the *whole* room (inadvertently, since he hadn't realized it was just for one). I didn't let on that we had already had words but told her that a family room would cost £50 for the night. She rang off, no doubt thinking we were all incurable cheats in the Borders.

Actually, what is even more irritating than the mean client is the person who reserves a room days in advance, and who turns up and stands in reception looking daggers, and asks to inspect the room before he or she takes it. Hell, they've already *booked* it! Imagine if I booked a room at the Dorchester, then on arrival asked to inspect the room first! What do I say to them if ever they *don't* take it? I know what I'd be thinking but I'd be told to wash my mouth out with soap if I said it!

If you take people from a voucher scheme, you may find you're trying to marry two tariffs. The first 'Roamin' Holiday' voucher guests we took paid good money for their vouchers in Holland, but we didn't get much for the voucher. Hence they came expecting the Hilton. Since we got so little for the voucher we tended to keep our smaller, though very pretty, attic rooms for voucher guests. These people had paid for more space than we gave them! Since our rooms were often blocked in high season by these low-paying voucher guests we don't do it anymore. Another voucher scheme which I joined recently—a scheme run by a German tour group—allowed me to dictate my own terms—5% agent's commission: this is a commission less than that charged by the Tourist Board, so it worked well and I didn't mind which room they used.

All this means you can't charge any old price depending on your whim, for you either won't get the custom or you'll lose it. You have to charge a fair price for the product and service you're providing. I always maintain that *you get what you pay for!* I like a bit extra comfort in my middle age and am prepared to pay for it. If I don't get it I'm like a bear with a sore head. Your guests will be entitled to feel the same. Beware!

CHAPTER 5

Reservations: taking bookings and registering guests
Diary versus Chart?

Most small hotels, Guest Houses and B & B establishments that are run by a husband and wife team use a diary to record their bookings. A diary can be bought at any newsagent in the high street, so it usually presents itself as the easiest solution. But there's a much better method, usually used by larger hotels. A chart is a far more efficient and accurate way of recording bookings. You can see a month's bookings at a glance. We use a chart since with diaries you can only see two pages at most and can misplace someone as you are turning the page. The chart system is so easy. See Fig 1 to see how it looks.

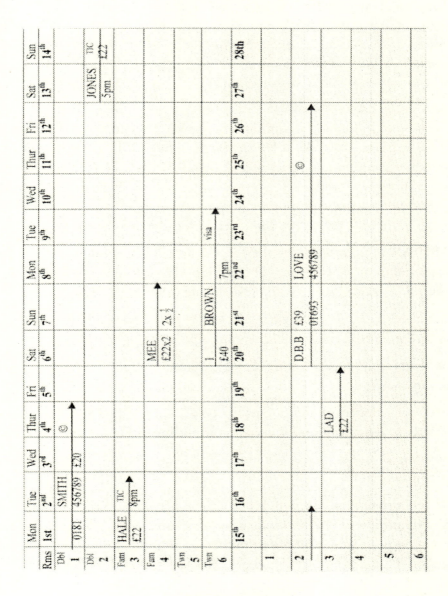

Fig 1: The Booking Chart

I'll explain our hieroglyphics. I'm assuming all these bookings were by phone, since they usually are.

Mr Smith is staying 1st to 4th inc., so I have drawn a line through the four days, ending with an arrow to indicate the end of the 4th (i.e. he will be departing after breakfast the following morning, on the 5th). His phone number is there as well as the amount he is being charged (per person). The 'c' means he has written to confirm.

Mr Brown booked by phone and gave his VISA number (I keep a notebook by the phone for recording such things). He said he would arrive by 6.30 so I gave him half an hour leeway—though I didn't tell him that. I told him that if he's going to be later than 6.30, then he should phone me to let me know (otherwise I'll let his room!). He's a single man so I've put (1) to indicate single occupancy of the room, and he is paying £40. He is staying from the 6th to the 10th, so I've drawn a line though these days.

Mr Jones was booked in by the TIC (Tourist Information Center) and is expected to arrive by 5pm. He is paying £22 (less the 10% commission the TIC take for themselves). He is staying from the 13th to the 15th.

Mr Hale was booked in by the TIC at £22 per person (a double room) to arrive by 3pm on the 1st of the month. He is staying 2 nights.

Mr Lad is staying two nights. This is a 'chance' booking. (He just knocked at the door!)

Mr Love is staying 7 nights, having booked Dinner, Bed and Breakfast at £39 a day. The booking has been confirmed in writing—hence the 'c.'

Mr Mee. Family room. 2 nights. 2 adults + 2 kiddies at half price. 'Chance'

Always write the details in pencil since you may have to transfer someone to a different room or someone may even cancel. Make sure you have the main details—name and phone number especially, so you can phone the person if his confirmation letter doesn't arrive and ask if he still intends to come. (Some people will just say in absolute amazement: "No, we're not coming anymore," as if you had some form of ESP; others will pretend they already phoned to cancel or have written and the letter got lost in the post!) Anyway, if you haven't had a letter of confirmation and there's only a week left before the person's due to arrive, then phone so at least you'll *know* what's going on. There's nothing more frustrating when you end up with an empty room (because of an invalid booking) when in fact you've been turning away bookings that might have filled the room again and again! (If a room remains unsold after the due date, you've lost the money you might have made from it forever!)

If the prospective guest hasn't got time to confirm in writing (he'll need at least four days), then get a time of arrival. Tell him (or her) to let you know if he's going to be later than the specified time so you can hold the room for him. He could of course assume from this that if he decides *not* to come, he can just not bother phoning—but it's a chance you take. Some just turn up as late as they please and expect the room to be waiting, with no idea they're two or three hours late. You may have let their room since they didn't phone. It's embarrassing but if you've a rule and you're confident you warned them, then it's *their* fault. We generally allow people about an hour after the time they specified. There aren't many phones on the last hour of the route here and they may have been held up by a tractor or a herd of lazy macadam-eating sheep. However, most people *will* phone.

We had one couple turn up a whole *day* early—I had them on the chart for the *next* day! The man was somewhat miffed but I did manage to fit them in because of a 'no show.' I checked their confirmation letter and indeed they *had* arrived a day early. It was Monday and they both thought it was Tuesday. They were horrified and relieved at the same time when I told them what day it was. (After all, it's not often you gain a whole day. The same thing actually happened to us when we were touring Australia. The distances were so vast that we felt obliged to push ahead. We had allowed two days to cover the distance between the Queensland border and Sydney and we did it in *one*—and forgot when, exhausted, we arrived late at night at our hotel near Sydney that we were booked in for the *following* evening. *We* were miffed to find everything closed up! But we found the owner and he was as patient and as helpful with us as we hope we are to *our* confused guests.)

Anyway, get their name, phone number, time of arrival or ask for confirmation. If you think there's anything odd about the booking (you get a nose for these things!) then put down the date the booking was made so if you come across it in a few weeks and there's no letter of confirmation then give them a ring pronto, for they probably aren't coming. Don't forget you can ask for a credit card number for confirmation: name, card number, expiry date (and time of arrival).

Our first year we had a gentleman turn up who was quite confident he had made a booking though none could be found. We had a spare room so we didn't contradict him—it didn't seem worth it. He stayed for a few days, happy as a sand boy and when he checked out he said "Thank you, Mrs Clark. I've been most comfortable." Jeepers! I had stolen Mrs Clark's guest. (Mrs Clark is the B & B lady up the road!) She must have been fuming as a result of her 'no show!' I never dared tell her. The irony is he came back a few times. I wonder if he ever realized his error? The moral is if you get people arriving insisting that they have booked and you don't have them on your chart, check they've got the right place. It's happened more than once to us. Maybe that's why the odd few guests of ours don't turn up—they're probably with Mrs Clark!

If you keep each chart then you'll be able to compare months as the years go by. You could even color in the various blocks or squares, after the day has gone, to see where your customers came from—i.e. AA could be pink, so color that person's room pink; TIC could be blue and so on. This way you can see at a glance where your guests have come from, and is a useful form of marketing information. At any rate, keep an eye on where your customers found out about you so you'll know whether your advertising is working.

Most people phone in their reservations, or fax, if you have one, or even E-mail their reservations if you have a web site. It's a bit awkward if they write and ask if you have a room for such and such a date since it may not be apparent if they're making a booking or just an enquiry. We treat such letters as enquiries unless they're specific and send a brochure with a letter saying whether we have the room and ask them to book if they want the room. When letters of confirmation arrive it's a good idea to reply promptly and personally if you have the time—just a line to confirm the reservations of a double or twin-bedded room with *en-suite* facilities, mentioning the date of arrival and length of stay, and adding that you're looking forward to their visit. This also gives you the opportunity to enclose one of your brochures plus any other leaflets you may have concerning attractions in the area. If you reply to the letters promptly (i.e. as the confirmations come in each day), then it won't be such a chore.

It's common practice to ask for a deposit for each booking. I know this makes common sense, since it protects you to some extent against a 'no-show' booking. Nevertheless, in our case we have preferred not to ask for deposits. Why? Simply since, unless we put the money in a separate account, we find that it has become absorbed into our cashflow before the guest has arrived! In other words, it feels as though we've spent the money before we've earned it—and that's disheartening. (It's a question of psychological motivation, I suppose.) Some people insist on sending a deposit and often feel their booking isn't valid unless they've sent you some money. In that case, by all means concur with their wishes. But normally, a written confirmation is sufficient to constitute a binding contract, and in the ten years or more that we've traded, only on a very few occasions have we had a 'no show' booking. It's heartening that, in our experience, people can generally be trusted! Anyway, if you get deposits then make a note of it on the chart and in your accounts so there can be no argument when someone says they sent you a deposit when they didn't. (We found that a deposit doesn't ensure the arrival of a guest—it just lulls us into a false sense of security. Once a guest booked two double rooms and sent me a Building Society cheque for as much as £40, and yet he failed to turn up.) Of course, if you take a decent deposit, say 75% of the full cost, then you haven't lost so much when the guest doesn't turn up. I suppose it's swings and roundabouts. A deposit should, of course, ensure the arrival of your guest. Most people do prefer the deposit system but, I must admit, I find it a pain in the proverbial dealing with piddly amounts of money.

Of course, it's not possible to get a deposit or a written confirmation for a booking made the day before, or on the same day as the date of the booking. In this case taking a credit-card number is advisable—though it's surprising how many tourists travel without credit cards. Invariably, for these last-minute bookings, one takes a risk—though asking for a phone number and for a time of arrival helps to reduce the risk. Invariably, however, there will be at least one 'no-show' booking each year—because one has taken a risk and trusted someone too far. You may fret and fume when the party concerned fails to turn up—but on the whole there seems to be little one can do about it. In our first year we had three double rooms booked for a group of people the next day. They had asked for vegetarian meals with goats cheese and other awkward things. I managed by some miracle to get all they wanted in town the next day. I prepared lots of salads and took great care in setting the table. It was the height of the season and I turned away other attempted bookings time and again. And yes—you guessed it—they *beep beep beep* didn't turn up! Of course, I had no record of a credit card or phone number—nor did I take an expected time of arrival. As Bereinstein bear would say: "That was lesson number one—don't get caught out again."

When the guest arrives, get him to check in—sign your book or fill in your registration card, or even just put his name and address on a piece of paper if you're feeling mean! He should do this before he or she goes to bed. It's not a lot of use waiting till the next day by which time he may have done a 'runner!' As I said before, you're actually required by law to do this and it's handy when you find a diamond ring by the bed to have an address to write to! It's also a way of asking the guest where he found out about you, since you can ask this on the form. Car registration number is also very handy!

Reservations are really very simple. Remember you need to cultivate a greasy telephone manner. Charles was so greasy one day on a booking from Holland that when the guest arrived the lady immediately insisted I drag Charles out from the kitchen so she could view this wonder she'd been so looking forward to seeing. He does actually have a lovely voice and he can be *so* charming. So, be as insincere as you like but *get* that booking!

CHAPTER 6

Fodder—feeding the herd! Breakfast
(They say it's the most important meal of the day!)

Having to feed your guests is probably the first thing to put you off buying and running your own place. It certainly daunted us. We must have bought ten cookbooks as soon as we knew the previous owners had accepted our offer!

Kindly landladies will tell you "It's just like running a large home—like running your own house, but bigger!" Well, it is and it isn't. If you make the eggs too hard, is your husband going to complain or send them back?

(If he does I suggest you swop him for a less fussy model!) If you forgot to buy the sausages and there's no milk left after the wee ones have raided the fridge, is your family going to walk out or complain to the Tourist Board? I doubt it.

Having said that, it *is* rather like running a very large house, with the difference that your 'family' is paying for their food and they're very fussy. This means you have to be a bit more organized and watch the quality more carefully.

Breakfasts are really easy. If you're not in the habit of feeding your own family eggs and bacon, then give them a treat and practice on them for a few days. Now I'll explain how it goes for us.

Breakfast for the guests is from 8 am to 9 am. We're downstairs in good time so there are no hiccups. (Coming down to a full dining room, having slept in, is a nightmare!) Charles takes in large jugs of fruit juice. If you have young people or Americans staying, you'll need to refresh this regularly. Put ice in to keep it cool. (Ice also improves the presentation!) We use orange and grapefruit since they seem to be the most popular. We use tetra-packs (1 liter) and sometimes dry juice like McDougalls Refresh to make them go a bit further. They're handy in emergencies since they don't go off. Juice will go off so you need to keep the juice fresh—don't just keep topping it up each day. Don't forget to leave glasses for the juice. Of course, you'll have put out the mini-portions of butter and Flora, jam and marmalade on the tables too! (Charles usually does this the evening before, when re-setting the tables after dinner.)

A large jug of milk sits on the buffet for the cereals. We put about 20 Kellogg's Variety Packs out (for variety, of course!), a large bowl of Corn Flakes since they are the most popular, and single portion packets of musli (Alpen—the second most popular cereal). Later I'll tell you where to get things.

The guests will help themselves from the buffet to juice and cereals. This will save you time while you're getting the breakfast cooked. The buffet also contains herb teas, Earl Gray (keep a jar of decaffeinated in the kitchen), saccharin, sachets of tomato sauce, brown sauce and mustard. You can use bottles but they get revolting if not cleaned each time. We also keep honey and marmite on the buffet. Really, the sky's the limit, especially if you want to impress the Tourist Board inspector! You could have peanut butter, cheese and fresh fruit. However, what you put out should reflect your charge. Remember that people can be wasteful if offered too much. Don't forget to provide the bowls for the cereals and, if you provide them, grapefruit segments. Keep a few tins of grapefruit, mushrooms and tomatoes in stock just in case.

While Charles is preparing the dining room (setting out the milk and fruit juices) I pre-cook the bacon and sausages. I can get about 8 slices of bacon (I use smoked back bacon which the guests love) under the grill at once. I cook one side, then put it on one side ready for the order. Generally two slices per guest. I keep the bacon in the freezer in 1 lb. packs. (Take it out at night so it's defrosted in the morning. I also take sausages out the night before.) I tend to use catering sausages since they look better and don't burst all over the show and curl every which way. I only use pork now in case any of the guests are worried about BSE. I pre-cook the sausages since you can't cook them properly to order—they wouldn't cook in time. You must be very careful that your meats are cooked thoroughly. To stop the bacon curling under the grill I use kitchen scissors and slit half an inch into the rind in about four places. This way it cooks properly and looks bigger, not having curled up.

While this is going on I also half-cook the tomatoes. I give mine a couple of minutes in the microwave to soften them up a bit so they grill nicely to order. I also keep a few tins in the larder just in case.

One could give fried bread, black pudding, beans, mushrooms, kidneys, kippers (I keep a couple in the freezer just in case) and so on. We've found that eggs (done in their various ways), bacon, sausages, tomato and haggis make a good full breakfast. (Yes, haggis goes down well in Scotland, even for breakfast—though mainly for the benefit of the tourists, mind you!) The health authority asked us to cook the eggs well. This is a bit awkward since most people like them just a bit runny. If I have surplus mushrooms, they go in too. I keep a tin of mushrooms in case they're asked for, though tinned mushrooms aren't really nice.

Now, back to the haggis! Obviously the reason we do haggis is because our hotel is in Scotland and people need to flavor the local produce. If they don't have it here, then they may leave never having tasted it. I buy it in the huge sausage form, slice it and freeze it till ordered. It defrosts quickly in the microwave and cooks in the 'sausage pan'—an old 'slow cooker' that once belonged to my mother-in-law in South Africa. (How intrigued she would be if she knew her pan would end up in Scotland cooking haggis for American tourists!) It cooks slowly, as the name suggests, and is perfect for sausages and haggis. The haggis arrives already cooked so just needs heating up. Always try to *do a deal* with your local butcher before rushing off to the Cash & Carry. Our chap is very obliging.

If you want to push the boat out a bit you could keep croissants in the freezer to order. It will take them about five minutes in the oven—people will just have to wait! In anticipation of American guests you could keep waffles, pancakes, muffins, and hash browns. You'll always have someone asking for something you haven't got. I'm rarely caught out—perhaps it's been due to good luck rather than good planning! Yogurt goes down well and porridge is sometimes asked for. Keep the two-minute cook variety in case someone wants it. Someone actually asked me for a pint of beer a while ago for breakfast. There's always a first.

You'll find that Americans are aggressive consumers and work hard at having a good time. Breakfast is no exception. They're fanatical about health and will demand only healthy options at breakfast. I can only assume they eat Mars Bars by the dozen in secret, since you don't get to be their size eating healthily! Charles, in his capacity as breakfast waiter, will say: "Full Scottish breakfast? Eggs, bacon, sausage, tomatoes and haggis?" and they will reply: "Yes, I'll have an onion omelette please with ham and pineapple." I promise you, he never mentioned omelette in any form. If you have the time and inclination to give them what they want, then they'll be pleased; but if you don't, then just be polite and say you're sorry but it isn't available.

Charles gets the order and asks if they want tea or coffee. (Charles took a pot of coffee to a lady and she said he had brought her tea by mistake. He didn't argue but came and asked me to taste it. It was definitely coffee. He made another pot, exactly the same as the first and took it in to her. "Perfect, thank you!" came the reply!) He invites them to help themselves to cereals and juice. He gives me the order (on a slip of paper torn from an order pad) so I can cook the breakfast while the guests are having their cereals. He puts brown and white toast into the toaster, makes the tea and coffee (don't use a cheap brand—you won't get repeats if you're stingy) and takes it through to the guests. That keeps them busy while I finish making the breakfast. By the time they've had their cereals and poured a cup of tea, breakfast is ready to go through. If you're a bit slow at first, don't panic: the guests are generally on holiday and not in a dreadful rush.

The smaller B & B where the lady of the house does it all herself often asks the guests the night before what they want for breakfast so she can be ready in the morning. It's really a case of thinking ahead and being ready. Don't leave a mad last-minute dash down to the hen hut to move the hens over to get the eggs when they should be in the pan. By the way, my best investment at breakfast has been a cast-iron frying pan—more expensive, but it doesn't stick and will last forever.

As I said, don't be stingy. In our experience people seem to value *quantity* before quality, though I wouldn't compromise on quality either. In all cases, rather increase your price a bit than cut back on food.

We generally get compliments about the breakfast, and guests say they don't need lunch after one of our breakfasts! But we learnt the hard way. This happened in our first year when my long-suffering husband took a breakfast in one morning to a man in a family group. The man handed the plate straight back, saying aggressively: "Please put some *breakfast* on that plate!" His wife's breakfast was about to go in so we just put her full breakfast on top of his full breakfast and made more for her. He seemed satisfied and ever since we've erred on supplying too much rather than too little.

We had the tiniest lady ever stay last year who had a full breakfast *(I can't manage one of our full breakfasts!)* and asked for an extra egg *and* some yogurt too!

Presentation is important. Don't throw the breakfast on the plate. Arrange it as far as possible in the time you have, and be sure to drain the oil off the egg. Make sure the table cloths are always clean. Keep salt and pepper topped up, inspect knives and forks before putting them on the table. Make sure crumbs (which will drive you up the wall) are not hanging about on the chairs or under the tables. Fresh flowers on the tables always make a good impression. I don't manage it in the winter at all and not always in the summer. It's a nice touch, though, and makes the guests feel you care.

Always check after the guest has had time to eat his breakfast that he's had enough. Does he need more toast or tea or coffee? Then leave them alone— if you can get away, of course. Some like to chat which is nice, but if you're busy or have bacon under the grill then it's more irritating than anything. We have some wonderful old ladies come and stay once a year. All I can say is there must be a lot of donkeys around with their back legs missing.

Getting away from the chatterbox can be quite difficult. We have a system of sorts. We have two telephone lines, one of which rings in the hall—so if one of us is stuck in the front the other can phone and just let it ring, giving the other a chance of escape in the form of answering the phone. I've had to be rescued from various parts of the house, bedrooms included, on a number of occasions by the children—they're fairly safe from the chatterboxes. We actually got to the point of drawing straws when certain guests require our attention. *I* always seem to draw the short straw! Don't get me wrong, though. We love them, but just haven't got the *time*. The expression used by a friendly guest, "Oh, breakfast is over, so you can go and put your feet up now"- wears a bit thin after awhile. To sit and have breakfast without interruption is a luxury—I should really get up half an hour early but something else will *always* fill the time and I'd still have breakfast after the guests!

Anyway, this is nothing to do with breakfast, is it? Come 9 a.m., all the guests have eaten. Well, most have. Sometimes people will try to sneak down after nine and there's not a lot you can do about it; but you can either give them breakfast, offer them toast and tea or just tell them to go away, they're too late! Recently a guest came down three quarters of an hour late so when he asked if it was too late for breakfast I told him *I* had eaten his breakfast. I gave him tea and toast and cereals. Still, it meant a delay in getting the dining room finished. We're too soft and the guests get away with murder. Sometimes guests will ask for breakfast early so one gives way, gets up at say 6.30 a.m. to wake them for a 7 a.m. breakfast. They turn up at 8 a.m., having gone back to sleep. And to add insult to injury, they don't leave till 10 a.m. Ggrrrr!

Two young lads came for the RAC Rally. This is in November and they were our only guests. They begged for an early breakfast so they didn't miss the first stage of the rally the next morning. I told them how often people asked for early breakfast but didn't mean it. "Oh, no, *we're* not like that. We won't let you down. We'll be at the table by 7.30 a.m." Okay.

Here goes again. 7.30 a.m. arrived. 7.45 a.m., then 8 a.m. I knocked at their door. "Are you having breakfast?" "Yes, on my way!" One lad turned up. "Sorry, my mate met a bird last night and he's not back yet!" His mate turned up at *9.15* a.m. Believe me, this pattern is not uncommon. I've taken to saying I want to see their luggage going in the car first. They'll want breakfast early, say 7 a.m., come down in reasonable time, eat, then they'll go to their room, have a shower, pack, mess about and leave at 9.30 a.m. What's *wrong* with people? Don't they realize that if they went through all their preliminary departure routine first they'd have breakfast at the normal appointed time anyway.

Some guests actually have breakfast between 8 and 9, pay their bill, then go *back to bed!* Naturally once they've had breakfast and paid I assume they've *left*. So when I barge into their presumably vacated room to collect the dirty linen it's usually quite a shock to find two heads with large eyes peering out from under the blankets. Charles blames it on the haggis. He has a theory that it produces an urgent aphrodisiac response—though generally it seems to have this effect on our younger guests.

We used to offer a continental breakfast in bed, but it really is such a hassle and people shouldn't really expect this service at the price we charge. We bend over backwards for the hunters because it makes sense—they *have* to be out before the crack of dawn. Also, I think one tends to bend over backwards for *nice* people—although one ends up going to great pains for the not so nice sometimes just to shut them up!

Just a reminder that if you use *real* wooden tables, have table mats *everywhere*. A lot of people don't have real wood in their own homes nowadays and don't realize that putting a jug of milk or juice on oak or mahogany does it no good at all, leaving those awful ring-marks as a testimony to past inconsiderate guests.

We have a friend who has one large table in her dining room so her guests *all* have to sit together and be sociable. She asks when they arrive which sitting they prefer, 8 a.m. or 8.45 a.m. Knowing our guests, they'd be all over the show (a good Yorkshire expression) but it works for her so will work for you if you don't have too many rooms. We have a table per room but one of our tables does four and another does six in case we have a family. You'll need a highchair too (this is where you *really* find out about crumbs and egg and cereals and, well, the whole breakfast on the floor).

Anyway, its 9 a.m. Sit down, put your feet up, have some breakfast yourself. You'll have to eat it cold since there will be interruptions—even if it's only just people checking out (or checking in!). Really, if you can, snatch ten minutes after the guests have gone. It's going to be a busy morning!

CHAPTER 7

Dinners (the easy way!)—*Bar* (hic!)

The most nightmarish part of a new hotelier's plans, unless you're a chef, is the dinner. It's one thing to cook for your family and friends, but quite another to do it for strangers. They are fussy and have likes and dislikes you can't imagine—*and* they're paying for it. You're serving up the sweet and the guest says, "Oh, by the way, I have a slight nut allergy!" At this point the temptation to place the chocolate nut pudding on his head is quite overwhelming.

I never regarded my cooking skills as spectacular. I don't even *like* cooking. (Goodness knows why I'm in this trade since I don't like housework at all!) Perhaps you feel somewhat intimidated by the thought of presenting *cordon bleu* dishes. Well, never fear—help is at hand!

We had some friends in Yorkshire who, just before we acquired our own hotel, had bought their hotel and we asked their advice. They said we could either cook it ourselves if we had the confidence, not to mention the time, or we could use a catering firm. We chose the latter—the easy way out—and it has worked very well indeed.

You might think this is cheating—to use pre-prepared frozen foods—but quite frankly, if a professional catering firm can do it better, then why not? I've recognized quite a few of the dishes we provide on the menus of places with proper chefs! I don't think any of our guests have ever realized that we use frozen dishes, except when the veg is frozen (I hate frozen vegetables and as far as possible prepare these from fresh), but even then they don't seem to mind. (Perhaps they're just being polite!) We buy our frozen food from Brake Bros. who also use Alveston Kitchens who, I think, are excellent. While these are a bit expensive, they're certainly worth it. (Address in the back.) The main reason for using these pre-prepared dishes is to liberate ourselves from being kitchen slaves. Remember, in a small hotel or guesthouse with, say, six bedrooms, you're not running a restaurant with a wide choice of menu. You have no idea in advance how many diners you'll have. You have to be able to conjure up meals of a high quality at *very* short notice—in many cases in less than half an hour. If there are only two of you running the kitchen and dining room, then professional pre-prepared frozen meals are a godsend.

Here's our menu as it stands at present. It's small, partly because this is slightly out of season and I don't want stock going old. When we first started we had a *huge* menu. It really isn't necessary if your guests are able to get to town easily for a meal if they don't like your choice. If you choose to encourage dinners every night in order to expand your turnover and thereby your profit, then you'll want a bigger choice. So here's our current (out of season) menu:

Starters: Prawn Cocktail. Soup of the Day.

Crispy Coated Camembert. Lentil & mushroom pate.

Main course: Salmon Paupiette. Beef Poivre.

Duck a la orange. Chicken Tarragon.

Desert: Ice cream. Treacle Sponge.

Dutch Cherry Pie. Chocolate Pudding.

We charge £17 for this. We vary it a bit but on the whole this is how it stays. What's more, apart from the soup, every item is provided by Brake Brothers.

Normally we request the guests to order at least an hour before they wish to eat so we can have enough time to prepare it. Dinner is 6.30 p.m. to 7.30 p.m.—the most popular time for our range of guests. If you leave it too late you'll never get sufficient rest in order to be bright and breezy when it's time to serve breakfast!

Just to give you an idea how *easy* it is:

The Prawn Cocktail is not a ready-made pre-prepared item, but the preparation is simple. Defrost the prawns, mix them in a prawn cocktail sauce and arrange on a bed of lettuce with a slice of lemon and some parsley. You could do them other ways, say in wine and cream. Imagine how you would like yours.

Soup of the day. I make soup for the family quite a lot but if there isn't any left then I use Campbell's condensed. It's the best quality. Don't use cheap stuff. Give a roll with the soup. You can get a box from Brakes with a variety of lovely rolls. I just pop what I need in the oven to defrost just before I serve.

Crispy Coated Camembert. Brakes again. It's lovely. Deep fry and serve on a bed of lettuce and garnish with tomato and parsley. Add a few neatly-cut slices of hot brown toast.

Lentil Pate. Brakes again. Defrost with a pat of butter. Scoop into small ramekins, garnish and serve with Melba toast (that's bread toasted normally, then split in half through the center to form very thin and delicate slices which are then grilled till brown). Very well liked.

The salmon, beef and chicken are from Brakes. The **duck's** from Booker Food Services since they have the Alveston Kitchens duck which is better quality. These all come in little pouches which you simply put in boiling water and about 30 minutes later are cooked—but watch out for the bags bursting or leaking. If there is, take out the offending pack and put in a new one (remember it hasn't been cooked for as long as the others). Keep it and give it to Brakes (or Booker Food Services) on their next visit and they'll reimburse you. If you catch it in time then you can always microwave on the setting they recommend on the box. Since the food is already cooked I feel microwaves might overcook it, which is why I prefer the boiling route. Garnish with whatever you feel is appropriate, such as two half slices or segments of a fresh orange for the duck.

Vegetables. We find those baby corn cobs are always well received and *petit pois* with *mange tout* can be defrosted from frozen very quickly if you're short of time. There's so much veg available it's really up to you. Fresh is best, of course, but if you don't know if you're doing dinners then you have to use frozen. We rarely know from hour to hour whether we are doing dinners, so inevitably we use a lot of frozen.

That was easy, wasn't it!

Ice cream. I make a butter toffee sauce to go with this or you can just squeeze some of that canned cream over it. Put in a nice spiral wafer and, say, an After Eight or whatever you fancy.

In our first year we went to a *lot* of trouble. Apart from the huge menu we did different vegetables for different main courses which really wasn't necessary. We made up little salads to go with various things; we even made our own chocolate rose petals (with our own rose leaves from the garden) to go with the ice cream. We did all sorts of things but we were worn out at the end of the year and realized that we had just gone too far.

Treacle Sponge is so popular we daren't take it off the menu; people even ask if we're still doing it when they book. It's from Brakes. Just defrost it in the microwave and pour Ambrosia ready-made custard over it. You could make it yourself, but it seems pointless when Brakes make such a lovely job of it. They do lots of goodies like this.

Dutch Cherry Flan. I chose this since it can be ordered after the main course has been eaten. We used to have things on the menu which had to be ordered when the main meal was being ordered since it took a bit of defrosting. A lot of people don't like to order their sweet ahead of time so now we have items that can be defrosted quickly in the microwave. If using a tart from frozen, make sure it's pre-portioned. Trying to cut frozen tart is impossible. Serve with ice cream or custard.

We give coffee and a mint afterwards and if you think people are still hungry (they generally complain they are too full!) then offer cheese and biscuits. This is a good test to ensure they're satisfied. I try to serve coffee in the lounge. It's more comfortable for the guest and you can then get on and tidy the dining room. For extra atmosphere you could put some music on but remember that PPL (Phonographic Performance Ltd) will want about £80 off you for this! You can put the radio on for free! I used to use 'real coffee' but was surprised to find so many people complimenting me on the regular I used in a hurry that I eventually stuck to Nescafe. Of course, its nicer with cream—but a lot of people prefer milk. At this point, if you have a bar, you could offer a liquor.

Some people request a meal when they book, arrive and we *never* see them again till breakfast. (This is another good reason for using pre-prepared frozen dishes! Imagine the waste if you've bought fresh food especially and spent all afternoon cooking their meal!) So, in short, we've learned not to cook anything in advance. Some come and find the price puts them off; others turn up having never mentioned a meal when they booked and want to have dinner. I think I prefer it when they just turn up and ask for a meal.

We sometimes do cheaper **short breaks** in the off-season. I don't use Brakes for this since their items are too expensive; and since these are pre-ordered meals. I cook everything fresh that day since part of the package is a set meal and I *know* the people are going to eat since it's a special offer—part of a package deal. ('Scarborough syndrome' again, did I hear you say? Bang on!) I keep the menu fairly basic, say, soup, roast beef, Yorkshire pud, and fresh veg might include cauliflower cheese and buttered leeks; this is followed by a pudding, say apple tart and custard, and coffee. Knowing they're coming for a short break gives one the confidence to buy things in advance. However, on our last session of short breaks we had two rooms booked for four nights. When the party turned up they found one old lady with them couldn't get up the stairs so they couldn't stay. The poor old thing could hardly walk. I think they were cruel to take her away. I found ground floor rooms for them at a competitor's. However, I had bought the food in for them for *four* days. What was I supposed to do with it—eat it myself? (Well yes, what else could I do with it?)

We had a few short breaks staying one weekend as well as our usual guests who order *a la carte*. One member of the short break party saw that others were ordering off a menu and said *he* would rather do that. This was after I had started to cook the meal. I asked what I should do with the food I had already bought and started to cook for *him*. "Should I eat it myself?" I asked laconically. "That's fine by me," he said as he proceeded to order from the menu! Irony, it seems, is lost on most of our guests.

You just can't count your chickens before they're hatched. If people phone and say they'll eat, that's fine, but don't depend on it! If you don't want to charge as much as us and you do your own cooking, which may entail a certain amount of preparation in the afternoon, and find that when the guests arrive they *don't* eat, then you're perfectly entitled to charge for the meal—even if they haven't eaten it. (Of course, one normally doesn't, for the sake of goodwill.) But you may wish to warn them you're going to charge. It's okay for us since it's in the freezer so nothing's lost if they don't eat—except for short breakers who can't get up the stairs!

Use your better plates at night. Dress the table up a bit with a candle or flowers. Use attractive wine glasses with colored napkins. Put on some relaxing music for atmosphere. Be careful here, though, since playing music to the public requires a fee paid to *two* licensing boards. (Yes, *really*! I didn't believe it myself at first either!) Their addresses are in the back. (By the way, if you have TVs in the bedrooms you should also pay towards a music licence. This can be extended, at an additional cost, to cover the music in the dining room and/or lounge.)

Brakes do a whole host of different foods. You don't have to get the expensive stuff. They do palatable plain food too and light dishes which are great for a snack menu. I would write off for their brochure. If you don't like cooking yourself, then this is the ideal way to serve good-quality professional meals. Also, as long as you keep the food frozen at the right temperature, it's probably the safest way too, especially as far as the Health Authorities are concerned.

We found doing short breaks early in the season starts us off slowly. I would never offer them in season since then we don't need the extra business. There are times when we almost give the food away in order to get the B & B business (Scarborough syndrome!). It's silly really, but after a heavy spending winter—last winter we took a six-week cruise to Australia—we often feel obliged to put a bit extra in the coffers.

For advertising see my *Marketing* chapter. The Tourist Board does advertise short breaks but we prefer to do our own advertising in a Sunday paper.

We find with short breaks that quantity is the *byword* if your price is cheap—say under £25 a head for DBB (Dinner, Bed and Breakfast!). Naturally one has to keep an eye on quality but a full plate means a lot to most short breakers, who are often retired people looking for cheap deals. We upped our price this year by only a couple of pounds and found the guests were a touch more sophisticated than before (they were friendlier and more appreciative!), and the generous amount of food we provided proved too much for them! We still asked if they wanted cheese and biscuits, but this was regarded as very funny. They actually get a *better* deal in a way since I give short breakers things like roast pork with applesauce, fresh vegetables and home made puddings! It's a grand meal, but short breakers generally prefer plain food. We tried things like prawns and pate but they weren't well received.

Doing these breaks involves a lot more planning, shopping and cooking. In fact it takes over your afternoon if you're not careful. Give me the ordinary dinners any time. But then, I'm a lazy cook.

Play about with prices and find your market—not too much, not too little. If the person you're feeding is on the large side, then be sure to give him or her extra! I didn't used to since I thought it was being rude, a bit too obvious as pointing to the person's weight. But my experience proves that large people prefer the option of choosing themselves, of choosing to leave food on their plates rather than feel hungry and unsatisfied! Who wants to go to bed hungry, after all? Our short breaks end in April. We always say we won't do it again but our fingers are crossed! It really is meant as a *top-up*. You need your time off and if you're trading below the VAT threshold then you don't want to over-earn in any one month—especially when you've got a heavy season coming up.

The best thing about doing dinners is it gives you a chance to get to know the guests since they like to chat as you come and go with the dinner. It makes a big difference to your goodwill and invariably they come back. There are some lovely people about and everyone has a story to tell. There are times when people just want to be left alone in private. It's best to be friendly but let *them* start the chatting.

Here's an example of when to shut up. We had a party of six diners. Only two of them were actually staying, the other four being *their* guests. As I'm used to being friendly and people responding to my polite remarks, I was surprised by their lack of responses. They were in fact a very dour party, the men making an effort but the women unwilling to join in. Anyway, when the couple staying checked out next morning they told me they had buried their son the previous day. I felt devastated. I also felt a fool when I remembered how I had tried to jolly them up.(Charles had even tried playing livelier music over the sound system. Eventually they asked for the music to be turned off!) Still, I suppose it was just as well I didn't know or I might have made the party even more morose. Make an effort—but get the signals right!

We used to do snacks as well as dinner. I suppose we still do but I don't advertise the fact. We used to put the snack menus in the bedrooms but hard work and getting too close to the VAT threshold has put a stop to that! We had quite a large snack menu: scampi and chips, curry, spaghetti bolognaise, toasties, lasagne, baked potato—generally things that could be popped in the microwave. However, this became somewhat exhausting since people would prefer the cheap snacks and want them at the same time I was doing the more expensive dinners. We were working flat out. We tried to keep the snackers in the lounge bar to save messing the tables in the dining room, but so many people wanted their bar snacks in the dining room. The snacks were very cheap and people took them as a cheap option, yet also asked for soup off the main menu as a starter *and* a pudding by way of making a cheap meal of it. We used to offer cheese and biscuits as an extra on the main menu for £1, but so many snack people got hold of the main menu and asked for *just* cheese and biscuits (yes, indeed, they would fill up for £1!) that we were obliged to take it off the menu. We've actually had people come to the kitchen door with tins of food, asking if they can come and heat them up in a pan. No, they jolly well couldn't! "Well, could you just boil this packet of spaghetti, then, while you're at it?" Of all the nerve—but I caved in and did it!

Basically, we're too small to do snacks as well as dinners. If you have staff who may as well be doing snacks as nothing, then it's a good idea. If not you'll be at it all night for very little returns. People have turned up at midnight expecting a snack. One thing you can count on—someone will *always* try to bend the rules. If you serve breakfast or dinner between certain times, people will always try to creep in earlier, or later. Try to be strict with your times—it isn't easy but hopefully (or hopefully not!) you'll get hardened to it. There's a good reason why landladies have a reputation for being hard! Having had a few years at this I realize why they do become a *type*. But they're only trying to defend themselves! Thank heavens 99.9% of our guests are wonderful.

We can't offer a lot of advice about catering staff since Charles and I generally run the show ourselves. Occasionally, when we have special parties in larger numbers than we can serve ourselves, we call in some part-time helpers who are friends rather than staff. But having worked on the front desk of large hotels, all I can say is *be careful!* I remember two women being sacked for trying to pinch two steaks each. The doorman searched them on the way out and they had steaks strapped to their thighs (the mind boggles as to why he was searching them there—I suppose it was a tip off!). We knew a chef who used to smuggle out whole cakes for his friends! When he served in the bar he gave drinks to his friends. We were dining out some time ago and the young waitress kept trying to take our plates away before we were finished; during pudding she confided that she couldn't wait to get home. Great! I can assure you this doesn't happen here, but in some restaurants staff take a wee bit of food off the plates they are taking into the dining room. In a restaurant my daughter was in the waitress came to the table to serve the pizza and hadn't noticed a string of cheese linking her mouth with the pizza. Can you imagine! In short, staff require a *lot* of watching, especially to obviate the problem known as 'shrinkage'—i.e. pilfering of food and drink. (Do you know how to mark your bar bottles so as to ensure the levels aren't falling unnoticed? With the cork in, turn the bottle upside down, and mark the level on the bottle in the upside-down position. That tip comes from an experienced barman!) So, if you've taken on a medium-sized or large hotel that requires staff, then be sure to set a good example and knock any bad habits firmly on the head.

I've mentioned our deals with a local restaurant before, and bears repeating here in connection with dinners. As I said, we used to do a deal for special breaks like New Year's and Valentine's night. We charged a decent price but we tried to give quality. We don't have a function room so we asked the local restaurant if we could take 6 tables for these special nights and worked out a price that included the dinner-dance at the restaurant. We then advertised the break with dinner-dance and explained to the customer on the phone that the break was in our hotel but the dinner-dance was just five minutes down the road. This worked out very well. You can do all sorts of things in the off-season if you want extra business.

We do special dishes for vegetarians if we are warned in advance and hope they turn up! Vegans present a bigger challenge since their diet is so limiting. I would actually recommend avoiding them if you don't need them. Sounds cruel but they're probably better in a big place that doesn't have to buy in especially. We once had a party of people booked in for a few nights. One of them was a vegan and clearly a person not liked by the rest of the party, judging by their joy when she cancelled. She sent us an intimidating list of likes and dislikes, which in a way is a good idea, except she was incredibly fussy. On the pudding bit she said she didn't want to be 'fobbed off with the perfunctory apple!' Well, who can blame her! Most people try to fit in. We had a diabetic staying for a week who didn't mention his condition till he went. Maybe it was best I didn't know. I don't like having to deal with people with food allergies since everything seems to have so much junk in it. I would refuse someone with a peanut allergy unless all they wanted was a jacket potato with salt!

American kids (who either tend or pretend to be precocious) are the worst to feed. It took me an hour and a half to extract an order out of a young American girl. Her parents were having the main meal and she didn't fancy that at all. She tried to choose from the snack menu (they could have gone to one of five restaurants in town but unfortunately elected to eat with us). She had to be cajoled into eating and the dialogue went something like this:.

"How about the lasagne?" I asked.

"Weeel," she drawled, scrunching up her nose. "How many layers has it got?"

"Three".

"Oh, I don't know. Is it mushy?"

"Not particularly—do you like mushy?"

"Yes"

"Then it's mushy".

"Oh, I don't know."

This went on through every dish: how it was cooked, whether it was too hot or too cold, whether it was steak mince or minced beef, what sort of cheese was in it, whether it was prepared with vegetable oil or 'that animal fat stuff,' whether the eggs were free range or not. It went on and on. Her mother pushed, her father pulled, her big sister told her she was a jerk (with which opinion I wholeheartedly concurred). Irony was coming fast and furious at the 60-minute mark. I was in and out between guests, hardly able to contain my exasperation. She ended up choosing the chicken goujons I had bought for myself for dinner later that night. I was overjoyed when she said she would have them and overwhelmed when the little madam only ate half!

Charles got his own back next day at breakfast. The dining room was full and he asked if she wanted the usual 'full Scottish breakfast' including haggis. She asked what haggis was. He took a deep breath and cleared his throat. (This was a frequent question from Americans and his answer is pre-prepared and practised as a result of having been recited many times.) He proclaimed loudly that it was a delectable mixture of all the parts of a sheep ordinary people in their ignorance don't have the good grace to eat and which they unthinkingly throw away—irresistible delicacies such as the heart, the lungs, the liver and the intestines. This, he said, after mincing into a delectable paste, is bound with oatmeal and wrapped in a sheep's stomach and enjoyed with unction. The whole room sniggered. What could she do but obediently say yes?

You'll find the odd guest wants a recipe from you. All well and fine if it's something you cooked yourself. Good idea to *know how* to prepare and cook the item you're serving!

We have a small wine list with prices to compare with most of the local restaurants. I get the type of wine I feel our guests are used to drinking. We don't do half bottles since they're hard to come by in this area. We offer wine by the glass. You'll need a table licence for serving wine. (Our licence in the Scottish Borders comes under the heading of Restricted Licence. See chapter on legal matters.) At present we charge £8 to £12 a bottle and £1.50 a glass. Some people just want a jug of iced water. Some popular wines we provide are Liebfraumilch, White Rioja, Niersteiner, Piesporter, Cotes du Rhone, Cabernet Sauvignon, St Emilion, Anjou Rose and Lambrusco Rose.

Bar

Having just a Restricted Licence we aren't allowed a bar as such. The bottles aren't meant to be on display, so we have a small dispense bar. We get around the problem by using a built-in cupboard behind the reception desk—a cupboard we normally keep locked. The glasses are kept under the reception desk. When people want a drink I simply open up the cupboard door, revealing the bottles and optics, and I generally leave it open for the evening—unless the drink is a one-off. I have Whisky, Gin, Baccardi, Vodka, Brandy in optics on the wall with sherry, port, Remy, Martini, Rum, Malts, Baileys, Tia Maria, Benedictine, Drambuie, Grand Marnier, Contreau on the shelves. Cans of lager and beer sit on the next shelf with mixers like Coke and lemonade. We have to display a notice that we're not allowed to serve drinks to anyone under 18. The Restricted Licence also means we're not allowed to serve drinks to anyone who is not resident in the hotel unless they are guests of residents and the residents are paying for their drinks. (An outsider or non-resident guest may also order a drink if it's accompanied by a meal!)

The measure you choose for your optics must be the same as the hand measure you use and the measure you use must be on your price list. You can get optics and measures from the Cash & Carry.

What time you shut your bar is up to you. I've had parties stay up till 2 a.m. One party comes every year. Last time I left them to it, telling them to write down any drinks they had. The first year they sat up late I made an agreement that they had to have a late breakfast so I could sleep in! A lot of the guests I trust and I tell them to help themselves and write down their drinks rather than having to keep asking me. However, not a lot of people drink very much so it really isn't a problem. Remember, though, you have to get up to do breakfast, whereas they can stay in bed till the last moment.

We had one couple from Germany in our first year that dubbed themselves 'the German Drinkers.' They'd insist on our having a drink with them after dinner and that would lead to one more and another *and* another. This can be a problem since we have to clean up after dinner and set up for breakfast. Imagine Charles having to serve the full Scottish breakfasts in the morning with an almighty hangover. It was a condition he shared with at least *two* of the guests. (In fairness, however, we have to admit that the same couple, who rejoice under the names of Fred Ohnewald and Christiane Schacke, have won a firm position in our hearts as best friends: on their repeat visits from southern Germany they bring loads of schnapps, and we've given way to the pleasant routine of acquiring what Fred calls 'balloon heads' in the morning. We've returned the compliment and visited them in Germany, where our late-night sessions were renewed with more 'balloon heads' in the morning. At least when we're in Germany the position is reversed since there we don't have the problem of serving breakfasts.)

I think the main problem with lovely guests is one doesn't have enough time to enjoy them, especially if one is nursing a *balloon head* from the night before!

CHAPTER 8

The Kitchen—where it all happens!

Not a very inspiring topic but probably worth a few lines, especially since the kitchen is the heart of your business. In most small establishments the kitchen table even becomes your office, the nerve center from which you run the whole show. This is certainly where you'll spend most of your time. Even our telephone lines, and the fax machine, are routed to the kitchen.

If you're taking over a going concern then you'll probably have to make do with what's there at first. We did. You'll find the cupboards *full* of somebody else's plates and other miscellaneous equipment. I would say don't throw anything away at first. Trade for a while—then dump things as the muse takes you. Actually, you may find some interesting objects which appear to have no use. You could use them as a party game, 'guess the objects use' and see how inventive your friends are. Does anyone know what you do with what I can only describe as a miniature man trap? (Someone speculated that it was an item for slicing pastry.)

I paid £300 for stock in hand. Not a lot—but as I went through the larder and found things like flour with a sell by date of two years previously, £300 seemed a lot! Most of the perishables were dumped as the weeks went by.

Dishwashers

We put in our own dishwasher, so now we have two. Some may say two is somewhat excessive for a place our size, but we weren't just going to sell ours so we whipped out a cupboard and in it went. We never regretted it. When we're busy we use both, especially if we're doing dinners. There was one night in the first year when we were so incredibly busy (people even came from a neighbor's B & B to dine!) that we harnessed Angus, our 8-year old, to help clear the tables in the dining room and lounge. Both dishwashers were so full we passed dirty dishes out of the kitchen window to Angus who stacked them in the back yard. If we'd had a visit from the Health Authorities that night we'd have been closed down! That was a one-off and we learnt to say no to outside trade. We bought a new dishwasher when one packed in—a 'hot-fill' dishwasher, so-called because it runs off our hot water which is heated by gas. (The electricity bills were horrendous—more about this later.) It has many settings and is quiet and quick. I would certainly recommend a dishwasher of this type. (It's a Moffat 31HF.) We replaced our second dishwasher with another 'hot-fill' machine, an Ariston LS601, though it has a design fault in that our largest dinner plates won't fit in properly. Something to bear in mind when buying a new one.

The cooker

We took over a huge electric cooker. It only had four hot plates but had a lovely griddle on one side with a small oven under it. But it 'leaked' electricity and to be fully off had to be turned off at the mains. It blew up one day (thank God) so we replaced it with a gas cooker. Electricity is a very inefficient way to cook, especially at breakfast time, since the grill and hot plates are constantly going on and off. Use gas if at all possible—it will save you a fortune. It's also quicker because it's a supply of *instant* heat. Our present gas cooker is a bit small when we're doing roasts for short breakers, but generally it's a vast improvement on the old electric cooker. Make sure your cooker is big enough to cope with the demands of a busy hotel kitchen.

Microwave ovens

We inherited two microwaves, a Moffat commercial oven which is still going strong though long in the tooth. Altogether we have three microwaves, which are invaluable—especially when you're dealing with frozen foods. If you're using frozen food a lot then one is not going to be enough. There have been times (when we've been doing snacks as well as dinners) when even three hasn't been enough! We still have three but don't use more than two most of the time. Really, the commercial brands are a much better bet, having more power with a longer life span.

Deep-fat fryers

We inherited two which were old and soon gave up the ghost. Now we have three new fryers, one for bitty things like scampi, a back-up and our regular 'household' one. All I can say is be careful and make sure they're out of the reach of kiddies and set in a safe place. Our kids aren't allowed in the kitchen when we're doing dinners—they'd be in the way and it's dangerous.

I have a Braun Multipractic **mixer and cutter**. I don't use it every day but its great for making bread, chopping vegetables for soup and the like. This is not an essential piece of equipment and I'd get by without it if necessary. I have the usual hand mixers and liquidizers that most homes have.

Toasters will drive you up the wall! On the whole I would say you get what you pay for. The more you pay the better it will do the job and the longer it will last. We use two which is really necessary. If one goes, get another the same day. If all the guests come down at once then one isn't enough! If your toaster takes to burning the toast, the biggest irritation will be the fire alarm. Our fire alarm is very efficient. You don't want it going off if guests are trying to sleep in or are still in their pyjamas. We bought a Salton toaster a few years ago and it proved to be quick and efficient. The latest one is a Swan 'Mellow Yellow' and is going just fine—for now.

You should have two **sinks** situated separately—one for cleaning food and one for cleaning hands. Ideally you also need one for cleaning large pots that won't fit in the dishwasher. If you're thinking of ripping out the kitchen and starting again then it would be worth your while asking one of the local Health Inspectors to come in and help you plan it. May as well get it right at the start. I'd love an impersonal stainless steel kitchen that's easy to clean.

Freezers

We inherited two. We had one of our own plus a large fridge-freezer. They're of the stand-up variety since there isn't room for a chest freezer. One guest wished we had one. He rented a beat on the Tweed for a week and paid quite a lot for it. He caught nothing for the whole week, but in the last 15 minutes he pulled out a 12lb-salmon! He was so excited that *we* were excited, and it certainly *was* a magnificent creature. Anyway, he asked if I could please freeze it so he could take it home the next day. Fine—but it wouldn't fit in the freezer without my having to bend its tail a bit. The fisherman was mortified when he saw his fish the next morning—with a permanently bent tail! I wonder if it really mattered. (Surely it will have bent back on being defrosted?) Anyway, requests to freeze the catch of the day are becoming more and more common. Expect these if you live in a fishing area.

Keep in mind **hygiene** at all times. Health laws are strict and you mustn't put your guests at risk. Keep food cool. Have a thermometer in the fridge. The fridge temperature should not rise above 5 degrees C. The freezer's temperature should be -18 degrees C to -21 degrees C. Don't let eggs get warm and watch their sell-by date. Have lots of J-Cloths so they can go in the wash each day. Have lots of cutting boards for different jobs. No animals in the kitchen. It's all common sense really, like placing uncooked meat at the *bottom* of the fridge, not higher up where it can contaminate foods on lower shelves. I'll mention a Health course in another chapter. Also, you can't do your laundry in the kitchen. That must be reserved for a separate room from food areas.

As I said, the kitchen is rather a boring subject. I'd like to keep as far away from it as possible and can only suggest you do the same. May I suggest a nice warm spot in the garden with a beer as a better alternative!

CHAPTER 9

To sleep, perchance to dream—or in plain English, **Bedrooms!**

What can I say about bedrooms? Family-sized bedrooms are best since you can fit more people in. We have two twin rooms. (If foreigners ask for a double then check they really *mean* a double since they may mean twin. We got caught out when a double was booked and in walked two burly men who would no more sleep with each other than I would with a grizzly bear.) We also have two double rooms and two family rooms. Obviously the size of the room dictates what type the room it will be. If your room will take a family, that's fantastic for then its use can have maximum flexibility—it can be occupied as a twin, a double or a family room.

Ideally a family room should have a double (or queen-size) bed and two single beds so it can accommodate a family of four (usually the parents plus two children). It may not be large enough for two single beds, in which case you may have a 'put-up' bed that's housed under the single bed. It comes as a unit with the single bed and is a bit costly but well worth it. Camp beds aren't very comfortable and don't make the right impression. Our 'put-up' bed has a proper mattress and base.

The state of the **beds** is very important. If they're old they'll sag and a guest who hasn't had a good night's sleep will no doubt complain, and he certainly won't come back. Experience tells us that most guests prefer a medium to hard bed. We did have one complaint that a bed was too hard but we have so many people tell us how comfortable our beds are that we know we've got it right. It's a case of personal preference, really. I prefer a softer bed, but most don't and there's not a lot you can do about the 1% who like to be different (except shoot them in the knee!). Don't let your mattresses get too old. The base will last longer than the mattress so if you're feeling a bit tight for money just get a new mattress at least. Turn the mattresses regularly. It will make them last longer and stop early sagging. It may sound daft but I vacuum my mattresses from time to time (twice a year!). Even with mattress protectors, which need regular washing, the mattresses must pick up a lot of dead skin.

Our family rooms have queen size and single, or king size and single. We brought the larger beds with us and they've proved to be popular. If you have an extra large room then a queen-size or king-size bed in lieu of a standard double bed is a bonus for the guests. There are a lot of tall people around. When people phone us and ask for 'the room with the bed,' they mean the room with the extra-large king-size bed. (It's an unusual bed with a wide decorative headboard, originally imported from Africa. You'll find that repeat guests get to know your rooms by their different features.)

I use **mattress covers** on all beds (address of suppliers in back). It's easier to wash them and they fit properly, easier than a blanket that shifts around. You can get waterproof ones but I'm not sure they would feel very comfortable and, so far, nobody has wet the bed! I use fitted bottom sheets since they save a lot of tucking in and don't need ironing since they pull tight over the mattress. I had some top sheets made especially from Western Textiles (address in back) in polyester/cotton, which irons better than pure cotton. These go under the **duvet**. This saves a lot of laundry. Imagine having to wash (and iron), say, ten duvet covers each day, as well as your other laundry, not to mention having to pull them off and put new ones on. If your guests don't spill coffee or wine on the bed (or, heaven forbid, get sick on the bed!), your **duvet cover** will last a few days before it needs changing. You can have a rota system for duvet covers from different bedrooms being put in the laundry. Guests will expect a **top sheet** anyway. I had them made fitted at the bottom. It makes tucking in easier.

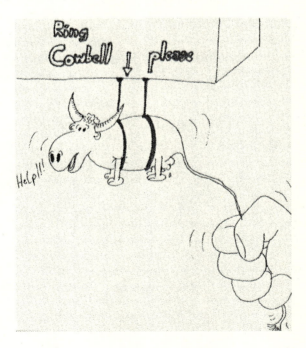

In our first year we didn't use top sheets. We simply laundered the whole duvet after each guest, which meant more or less every day. This made for a lot of washing. And, as I said, guests expect to see a top sheet. American guests, especially, would almost assuredly come down and ring our cowbell. 'There's no sheet between the bed and the comforter,' they'd complain. On each occasion we had to reassure them that we washed the duvet so that the top sheet wasn't needed. This happened so frequently that we gave way and bought top sheets for all beds. A good move, as I said, since it saved a lot of washing. Airing duvets in our climate isn't easy but do stick them out of the window if you can between showers.

I would always use good quality bedding with a high percentage of polyester since they last longer and the ironing is minimal. When you're viewing a place with a view to buying, check the bedding. Once we moved in we felt obliged to discard much of the bedding, for inadvertently we took over bedding that was worn out. It cost a fortune to replace it. You'll need a change of linen for each bed—at least two duvet covers, two bottom sheets, two top sheets, eight pillow slips (for a double bed), and eight towels (for a double or twin room). Having to replace all the linen in six bedrooms is going to cost about £2,000. Even your new things will get old and you'll need to keep replacing things. Watch they don't all wear out at the same time!

Try as far as possible to have the **curtains** match the bedding and the bedding match the wallpaper. (Don't use thin curtains or the guests will wake too early!) It looks so much better if things are reasonably coordinated. Presentation of bedding is as important in the bedrooms as presentation of food in the dining room! We had a woman complain in our self- catering cottage that the bottom sheet did not match the duvet (which matched the pillow slips and curtains)!

If you have room for a family then someone will ask you if you can provide a **cot**. Storing cots is a dreadful nuisance. You can get foldaway ones from International Hotels Supplies (address in back). If using your own just check for safety features.

We have a **color TV** in each bedroom. This is standard now. We don't pay any extra TV Licence but we do have to pay about £83 to the **Performing Rights Society** (address in back) though I would be tempted to wait till they come knocking at your door first! We rented the TV's at first but after a few years bought them off the rental company. We always have a spare just in case. If I'm doing the bedrooms I put the TV on; it eases the boredom and I can check the TV at the same time. If you're short of room you can always put the TV on a wall bracket.

Hospitality trays are also standard. Cup and saucer and spoon for each person. A glass. We use plastic tumblers instead of glasses since they tend to be taken into the bathroom. If they got broken you'd be taking an awful risk of guests cutting their feet. We give a packet of biscuits. Get mini packs from the wholesaler. We give two of everything for each person—tea bags, coffee sachets, coffee creamer, white sugar, brown sugar, powdered milk for tea (I sometimes offer a jug of fresh milk when they arrive if I have the time). All these items come from Booker Food Services or the Cash and Carry. A small teapot is a good idea. Check the tray each day. Some obliging people wash the cups themselves in the bathroom and you won't know they've been used unless you check the number of sachets used. I once heard a young man say that he worked in bedrooms in a large hotel and instead of taking the tray to the utility unit where he was supposed to wash the cups and refresh the tray he just licked his finger and rubbed it round the cup till it came clean. Did you just feel a shiver going down your back? Give me a small hotel any day! You can get a ready-made tray in plastic which will attach to the wall. Handy if you're short of space. (Address of supplier in the back.) They're a lot tidier of course but then again are very plastic. Don't forget a kettle. Nothing huge, but it should be automatic. By the way, make sure all your plugs are firmly attached to their wires and not wobbly where the wire goes in. Make sure there are no exposed colored wires. It's something the health inspector will make a point of looking for.

If guests come and ask for extra condiments—coffee or sugar sachets, or whatever—*don't charge them!* It really makes you look mean and will cost you your goodwill.

We provide **luggage racks**. (The Tourist Board will require you to have them for certain grading levels.) I think the ones that fold up are the tidiest and take less room. You can get them from International Hotel Supplies (address in back). You could fix one to the wall. In other words, ask your joiner to make it for you in such a way that it can be used as a seat as well. Have the wood on good brackets that fit against the wall, so it can be folded back with retractable legs.

As I said, a luggage rack is an item the Tourist Board will expect.

Not everyone likes a feather **pillow** and allergies abound, so make sure your spare pillows are hollow fiber or something similar. I also keep spare blankets in the wardrobe.

Try to have good quality **coat hangers** though I'm afraid they *will* disappear in time. Guests take your good ones and leave cheap wire ones in their place. In our experience they're the only items that go missing, except for shoe-cleaning equipment. A solution will be to have hangers that are tailor-made for your wardrobe, where the hooks are detachable and remain permanently fixed to the rod. (Once again, these are obtainable from International Hotel Suppliers. See back of book.)

You could provide a **clock** or even a **clock radio** but you may have guests complaining that they were woken too early by the alarm set by the person the previous night!

Tissues are a nice touch but they'll disappear quickly.

I used to leave the **shoe cleaning equipment** in the drawer of the dressing table but they disappear so rapidly that I keep them downstairs: guests are very welcome to come and ask for one. Each costs nearly £1 which at the end of the day mounts up. I used to leave tins of polish and brushes but it smelled of polish and if it got on the sheets then a lot of cursing was called for. The least negative energy expended the better.

A **notice** in the room about times of breakfast, dinner, extra facilities like the use of an iron and hair drier is a good idea. My notice also mentions that 10.15 a.m. is the latest checkout time. People (especially continentals, for some reason) will stay half the afternoon if you let them! (One competitor turns the electricity off at 10 a.m. if they haven't gone!) If it's convenient I ignore them, but if it's gone 10.15 and they're holding me up then I tell them they must go so I can do the room for a new arrival. It's always awkward when people are staying on and you want to clean the room and they just won't go out. You find you're popping up to do their room at 2 p.m. which should be your time off. I now put a comment on my notice that rooms will not be serviced after 10.30 if the room is still occupied. You can always leave clean towels and a loo roll and even a fresh hospitality tray outside the bedroom door if they don't want to leave the room.

We leave **Bibles** in all the rooms. Phone the Gideons and they'll gladly come along and do it for you. I leave magazines in the lounge and guests are welcome to take them to their rooms. The Tourist Board hand out '**bedroom packs**' early in the season. These are handy for local information and are kept one in each bedroom.

Good idea to leave **menus** from local restaurants and pubs in rooms and in the lounge, unless you want them to eat in of course!

I suppose this is a good time to mention **bathrooms**. Each person is gong to want a good sized **bath towel** and a **hand towel**, and some like a **face cloth**. I buy the soap in bulk from Booker Food Services (they provide a lot more than food!). I buy the cheapest since it has to be replenished every day. (I know a few ladies who's establishments have a Highly Commended or Deluxe grading who buy expensive soap wrapped in paper for each guest. I have to admit, to go to this expense for soap that has to be discarded each day seems a frightful extravagance.) A **bath mat** is important for comfort and to keep your carpet dry. We did have tiles on some of the bathroom floors but they got a bit loose and there was a danger of guests cutting their feet so we put carpets down instead. Really, it's not a big expense since there isn't a lot of floor to cover. **Toilet rolls** of course. We try to keep a spare in each bathroom to obviate the risk of guests being caught short and the inconvenience of their having to come down and ring the long-suffering cowbell for a new toilet roll!

We go through a lot of toilet rolls, but the strangest thing is we also go through a lot of toilet seats! In fact, Room 1 had so many problems we thought the loo must be haunted.

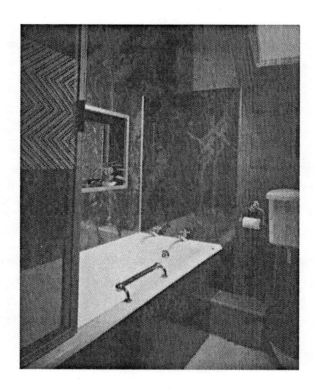

Bathroom with Scanform panels

We have had all our bathrooms *Scanformed*, something which I would certainly recommend. This involves placing washable waterproof panels over your existing ceramic titles, or using Scanform panels in lieu of tiles. The only joins are at the corners of shower cubicles, so there is virtually no possibility of mildew building up as it does between tiles (and which has to be got rid of with an abundance of elbow grease and bleach). The tiles get so grubby and they need re-grouting so often! You'll need to ask your local joiner about this if you get 'tile-sick'! (You may use Respatex panels instead of Scanform panels. They're basically the same product.)

You'll need a **wardrobe**, a **bedside table** for each person with a good-sized **reading lamp**, a **chest of drawers**, a **mirror** for make-up and a **full-length mirror** for admiring one's whole self. Also, a couple of **chairs**, the more comfortable the better.

Make sure the windows open. The guests will want to control their own ventilation and if there's a fire they need an alternative exit to the door.

My parents actually stayed in an hotel in Whitby where the fire exit was through their bedroom. The landlady said they mustn't leave the key in their bedroom door at night in case there was a fire. A spare key for their door was in a glass case outside their door. They had images of other guests frantically rushing over their bed in the night.

Pictures on the walls make the room so much friendlier.

We have **radiators** in all the bedrooms plus an electric heater. Electric **heaters** are best fixed to walls if convenient; they're certainly safer that way.

If you allow smoking in bedrooms then keep **two ashtrays** per bedroom all the time—though we've had guests put their cigarette butts out on the plastic hospitality tray despite the fact we provided ashtrays in the room. One can at least try.

For the guest the most important room is the bedroom. They're going to spend at least eight hours in it so make an effort. People complain but a good many more give compliments. If your bedrooms are comfortable your guests *will* thank you. (I can't recall how many times guests, on checking out, have thanked me sincerely for a wonderful stay. And yet in most cases I don't recall doing anything at all. Clearly it's the bedroom—your sleeping partner—that did the job!)

CHAPTER 10

The epitome of boredom—Bookkeeping!

The little heading in our notebook for this hotel guide says 'Bookkeeping is easy'! Yes, it is for Charles—he doesn't do it, so no wonder he finds it so easy! Well, if to me it is, to many it's a positive minefield not to be entered at any cost.

Never fear. It can be as easy or as difficult as you care to make it. I decided to go 'middle of the road' difficult, if you know what I mean: easy, but not so easy for the tax man should he come snoopin'. No, but seriously—my side of the bookkeeping is relatively easy since I only do enough to provide my accountant with the essential details he needs for submitting my accounts for tax assessment. No doubt my accountant is very clever, working out my hieroglyphics. I leave little notes all over the place explaining why CD's should come under hotel business and not under personal, and so forth. On our last visit to him he said quite categorically he'd never had a client with so many bank accounts! Well, if we move money around fast enough and often enough it will even confuse ourselves. A few other little businesses came out of our hotel enterprise so more than two or three accounts were called for.

I believe if your accounts stay under £15,000 per annum (rather difficult in most cases) then you don't need an accountant to represent you, in which case you can DIY. I do a basic day-to-day bookkeeping of money coming in and going out, balance it at the end of each month (for my own peace of mind as much as anything), and hand it with receipts, bank statements, etc. to my accountant at the close of my tax year. (You can choose from which month to begin your 12-month tax year. Isn't that thoughtful of the Tax Department? You see, we live in a democratic system where we, as business folk, enjoy the benefit of all kinds of freedom, flexibility and concessions. We even have the power to appeal against a taxation we might consider too high or unfair. Thank God we don't live in a straight-jacket system where the hotelier might develop an authoritarian conscience—one where the heart misses a beat at the mere mention of HMS Inspector of Taxes, or the IRS which can reduce the businessman to an ineffectual quivering lump of jelly!) An accountant provides the essential role of a buffer between the tender and vulnerable hotelier and the tax department. Hence, in our case, it's our accountant who prepares the official set of accounts for the tax man (bless his heart!) as well as for us. We also send our tax returns to him and he takes care of all that horrid form filling, which he says is easy! I'm absolutely positive you save money in the long run by using an accountant. The money he saves you pays for his services. Also, to be in bad odour with the tax man is worse than your worst nightmare. (Our window cleaner told us recently he had a chat with his tax man who advised him not to do his own accounts but to use an accountant because an accountant has more credibility. It appears that in time past, out of choice, he wasn't working a full week and naturally didn't earn as much as the tax man would have expected, so that the limited amount of his declared income looked suspicious.) By the way, you must keep all sets of accounts for at least seven years, so don't be hasty in throwing away any of your records.

There are lots of accountants. Look in the Yellow Pages, or better still, ask for recommendations. Phone around and question them since you'll be paying them for their services. Find one that already has a small hotel on their client list so they have experienced hotels' 'little ways.' Go for the best—someone who's 'chartered,' someone wholly *qualified*. We pay around £900 a year which at first glance seems awfully high, but using the services of someone not really qualified, albeit cheaper, would be to open a veritable Pandora's Box of nightmares. Be careful, for someone recommended by someone else is *not* always the right move! Check them out first. We first thought our accountant's fees too high so, on the recommendations of a plumber we once used, we transferred to a bookkeeper. We were charged £700, less than the accountant's fees, but the whole thing led to such a nightmare with the tax department that we went back to our accountant so he could sort out the mess. So, in the end, we paid almost *double* that year.

Anyway, this is more or less what our accounts look like. I use a 16 column account sheet rather than a formal book. It's cheaper and if you make a mistake you can always start a new sheet. I keep my month's sheets in a cardboard file which stays in the kitchen since I do all my paperwork in there. (You see, I *told* you the kitchen was the heart of the business, didn't I?) The bits of grease and food that stick to it over the months give it real character. On the back of this file I note useful things like mortgage roll number, various insurance policies, their names and numbers, what they're for, how much and when they're paid. It's so much easier to note these things down as you start the policies rather than having to hunt through files when you need them.

At the end of the year I do a summary of each month end. This isn't really necessary, but it gives me a good *overall* view of how each month went—what we spent on food, advertising, electricity, repairs. It's reassuring (and sometimes depressing!) to see just where the money went.

Petty Cash

Give yourself a 'float' from the business account. £30, £100, that's really up to you. Keep a note of all cash spent and keep receipts. At the end of each week tot up the receipts and check that the cash you have left is less the amounts of the receipts and mark it into your 'money out' sheet under petty cash. You'll need to keep change for the guests anyway.

Creditors

I used to pay bills as they came in. Now I sometimes make them wait for as much as 28 days. This partly depends on when I get down to the paperwork. Try to keep on top of it and have a reasonable filing system. It's amazing how often one needs to refer to something in the files. The same day I pay a bill I write it into my 'moneys out' sheet and mark the cheque stub so I know it's been entered. I then put the invoice on a bulldog clip and keep it together with others paid out till the end of the month. After I've balanced the accounts sheets at the end of the month I put the invoices with them and they all go in a file marked for that month in the filing cabinet.

Debts

You shouldn't really have any. We have an arrangement with a couple of local firms to whom we send guest accounts. From time to time we have to chase them, though they always pay up. However, I wouldn't advocate allowing all and sundry to do this. Give the firm a limit allowed to owe in one month and if they ever let you down don't let them have credit again. No custom is better than bad custom.

VAT (Value Added Tax)

I wonder how much verbal abuse has been hurled at the VAT-man? He has the reputation of the Inquisitor and we have yet to hear a good word about him. So we avoid him like the plague.

At the time of writing the VAT threshold for small businesses is £48,000. That means you are allowed to earn up to that amount of turnover in any one 12-month period without having to pay VAT—i.e. if it's March 30th 1995, then you count all the month-end takings backwards to and including April 1994. If it's 28 February 1995, count all turnover back to and including March 1994. I hope you got that. I regret that ignorance is no excuse, so ask your accountant to keep an eye on you. I would recommend making an effort to stay a good £1,000 *under* the limit to allow for misunderstandings and mistakes. This may sound like nonsense. How can you *stay under*? It happens naturally with us, though our turnover could exceed the threshold if we cared to work ourselves into an early grave. It works like this for us: It's come to the beginning of November and you know that if you take another £2,000 you'll be into VAT. You're exhausted, your eyes are red-rimmed and your head is pounding. You *hate* people. You've been at it without a day off for 7 months—that's 28 weeks or 210 days without a day off. Most people in that time have had at least two bank holidays, three weeks annual holidays and 28 weekends, not to mention sick leave which we don't take. The hotel is looking in need of a good clean. You've got to start the decorating soon and catch up with a thousand jobs you've been putting off for the past six months. So, are you going to do short breaks (the Scarborough syndrome!) when you don't really need to—when you-ve put enough money away to get you through the winter, and when any additional money you make will mean getting into VAT? *Of course* you're not! So what are you going to do? You're going to close that front door and try to rest. (It's hard to rest at first since you've been in *go mode* for so long it's hard to sit down). If you've any sense you'll take a couple of weeks to recoup a bit then go off somewhere really wonderful for at least a fortnight since you know that if you're in the hotel you *can't* stop—even if it's just doing a bit of spring cleaning. In December you'll be getting ready for Christmas and Hogmanay. In January you'll be getting over Christmas and Hogmanay. The rest of January and February you'll be decorating and fixing up the chips in the wallpaper, spring cleaning *everything* in sight, having the joiners and plumbers and God knows who else in. March will see you wondering about taking short breaks which you really don't want to do and relenting in between catching up on paper work, tidying the garden, shampooing the carpets and trying to watch TV for an hour without interruption (bookings for the season are starting to come in). So, hopefully I've justified why we stay out of VAT—it's through exhaustion. We *have* to stop sometime and what better time than at the VAT level? A lot of sale particulars say that the owners have deliberately traded under VAT. I suppose this is what they mean, so you could say we deliberately trade under VAT. If it's not possible to stay under, then in you go—but give it some thought first. I wouldn't recommend going into VAT unless you can do so by a largish amount, since anything over £48,000 (or whatever the VAT threshold is when you read this) would mean paying around £8,400 or more to the VAT-man (i.e. 17.5% of your turnover). Say your VAT threshold is £48,000 and you do £50,000: then you're going to have to give yon VAT person £8,750; but if you trade under £48,000, you don't. If you're a small business, that could mean four to six weeks hard labor just to pay the VAT. In other words, if you're only going over by say £5,000, then consider whether it's worth it since the VAT-man is going to want that for himself. In which case you're working for him. I know you're able to claim back (claw back is the expression used and how apt that is!) VAT paid on some bills paid but it's highly unlikely you'd be in pocket unless you were doing major development and were paying huge VAT bills or intended to increase your turnover anyway. Some food is not VAT-able; ice cream is, napkins are, soap is, electricity is, bacon isn't. Who wants all that paperwork unless it's going to be worth your while? It must cost Mr Public a fortune each year to employ people to work out what is and isn't VAT-able

I think our most valid reason for staying out of VAT is the VAT-man's awful reputation. He's painted as the Grim Reaper by many small-business owners with whom we've spoken and has probably performed that act on more than one poor soul.

VAT presents a form of imprisonment for small businesses wanting to grow. The VAT threshold is a form of artificial constraint. Many a small business has gone under because of it. We had encouraged some friends through our enthusiasm to buy a small hotel in North Yorkshire (before we got ours). It looked like a good business, well into VAT. We were envious. They moved in during the high season. (Imagine never having done B & B before, moving house and having to do dinner for 12 all on the same day; *ye gods*, this lady was amazing! Moving in during high season is not to be recommended. We moved in 1st March. Ideal!) Anyway, these delightful people should have been very successful. They had a lovely place, great personality, and were able to conjure up superb meals—all the right ingredients. Yet they didn't even make it to the VAT level in their first 12 months. Unfortunately they had already registered for VAT since the previous owners showed a high turnover well over the VAT threshold On this occasion the VAT-man was sympathetic (I take back 1% of what I said previously!) and allowed them to de-register for VAT, after they had paid him their dues of course. Unfortunately this seemed to be *the stick that broke the camel's back* and they had to sell up. He went into the ministry and she is a free-lance journalist. The moral here is not to register till you actually need to or *know* that you're going to need to.

If you do go into VAT then this is where a really good accountant could save you hours a week. You need someone who is meticulous and who may even drive you up the wall wanting receipts and every penny accounted for, for this is how the VAT-man likes it.

If you do think you may well like more than one business in time to come then bear in mind your VAT situation. As far as VAT is concerned any similar businesses you have will be conjoined, or counted as one—i.e. if you have a guest house business taking in £35,000 a year *and* a B & B (or, say, two holiday cottages) taking in £20,000, then you are £7,000 over the VAT limit and will have to register (and pay VAT). (Both businesses are accommodation or hospitality-based, and are owned conjointly by the same partners.) However, if you have a spouse and put each business in a *separate* spouse's name, then you can run the businesses on a separate VAT basis (in so far as each spouse will be trading as a sole trader). In this case there would be no VAT. If you were to run a hotel and self-catering cottages then they should be run as separate businesses with separate title deeds under different names. It is the *person* who is registered, not the *business*.

Be up-front with the taxman, unless you have nerves of steel. We made 55% profit last year which is more than most people would show, but that's just the way it went so we showed it.

You'll find little ways around things if you feel justified. With our golf package we find that if the guest pays with one cheque for the whole deal then the *golf* (money payable to the gold clubs) also becomes part of *our* turnover. Well, that just seems unfair, so it's better to get the guest to send a separate cheque for the golf part of the package, made out to the Tourist Board rather than to us. What we're doing is not illegal. We don't offer golf in the hotel so why should we pay VAT on it?

We've decided to stop doing dinners after this year, which means we'll downgrade our status from hotel to guesthouse. This is mainly because we get tired and our free time means more to us than the relatively small profit we make on dinners. *Everyone to their own.* This of course will make the VAT situation a little more flexible for us since we do sometimes seem to get awfully close to the threshold. We don't turn business away to keep out of VAT, but if our prices went up and the VAT level didn't and dinners went up, which is what they will have to do eventually, then we'd hit it. If we worked in the winter we'd hit it. It's also fortunate that we do take a part of the winter off since one just has to close. As you will have seen already, this is a very demanding business and you need a few months to recharge.

The VAT-man probably regards our taking time off in the winter as cheating. We justify it through exhaustion!

There are many excellent computer programs, of course, to take the tedium out of bookkeeping!

CHAPTER 11

Repeat Trade—Knowing you got it right!

Getting your guests to come back is probably the easiest form of marketing you can do. It doesn't cost anything and is rewarding. You also have the satisfaction of knowing you're doing it *right*.

They will invariably contact you on the phone. Most introduce themselves properly. "This is Mr Smith. We stayed with you two years ago. Can we come back?" You aren't expected to remember them particularly well the first time—you probably won't! But invariably there's something familiar about people who've been before. Some just turn up at the door and you *know* they're familiar. Say so. "Hello! Didn't you stay here last year?" It may have been the year before but they'll be delighted you remembered. If you were wrong and they haven't stayed, then you've done no harm anyway.

It only gets awkward when the anonymous voice on the phone gushes:

"Hi! It's Jim. How *are* you?"

"Fine thanks," you reply, frantically searching your memory for Jim.

"Yeah!" the voice continues. "We want to stay for a week in the middle of June. Same room as before. In fact, we'll have the same dinners—that's if you still do dinner?"

"Gosh, Jim, it's lovely to hear from you. It must be a year since you stayed?" Try to get some information out of them.

"Yes, exactly same time."

Thank heavens. All I have to do is look up last year's chart. "It was Room 2, wasn't it?" (Hoping it wasn't the family room they'd slipped into by mistake.)

"I think so. The one with the huge bath!"

Great, that's room 2. "Well, that's super, Jim. I'll pencil you in. Just give me your phone number again. Save me looking it up. Let us know if you're going to be late. It'll be great to see you again. Just confirm in writing as usual. Bye!"

Just a little probing is much nicer than saying you don't remember them from Adam. It's amazing how often you *do* remember people. We all have our little quirks!

We have two old ladies who come once a year. They even called in for coffee when they were in the area. They need to be met off the bus, want a bowl in the bathroom since Avril can't manage the shower, they like warm milk with their coffee, and so on. The more quirks they have the easier they are to remember. These two were memorable from day one. They are

80 and 90 something. Their brains will surely live on long after they die since they're so bright and witty. I was going to say I wish I had their intellect when I'm their age, but I wish I had it *now*! They're avid readers and are always trying to catch Charles out on books he maybe hasn't read (he's an ex-Professor of English Literature). They must think I'm a total moron though I do pretend to read Mills & Boon or some such thing to make their hair stand on end! It's all in fun. They're avid talkers too. Once caught, you never get away. We take it in turn to answer the bell when they're here. Judith keeps saying, "Come on Avril, Jo must have loads to do"—but dear old Avril keeps going like a steam locomotive out for a Sunday afternoon run and thoroughly enjoying it, bouncing from one foot to the other. For all this, we love them, but would rather they came in the winter so we had time to talk, or rather listen. Charles is very mischievous and tells them how much Joyce, the lady in the Tourist Information Center, is *dying* to see them again! (Joyce complains they take up much of her valuable time singing Charles's praises!)

It's easier to get to know people if they're having dinner, since one chats between courses and a pleasant *rapport* can develop. However, a lot of our repeaters are very quiet and self-effacing and we hardly know they've been before they're back again.

I think you just have to be yourself. Be friendly, smile a lot (and mean it), listen a lot, and try your best to remember (and use) their names. Keep the place clean and comfortable. Let them know that you're there and that they won't be a bother if they want something (even if they are!); then you're well on your way to repeat trade. Create a welcoming atmosphere. Most people are amazingly easy to please. We estimate we've had about 18,000 through here in eight years and have had only three people complain. Of course that doesn't mean everyone was highly satisfied—just that nobody else had taken the trouble to let us know they were unhappy. If you do get a complaint, then deal with the situation, whatever it is, since you don't want a repetition of it.

Don't be stiff with people, unless they appear to prefer it that way. Pass the time of day, offer to help with the luggage, take an interest in them. Remember, when people arrive they're invariably tired from traveling and need to relax as quickly as possible. They may seem stiff at first but generally the stiffest guest is as soft as butter by morning after a good night's sleep. Some people are *too* self-effacing. We had a lady stay in a double room on her own. Her son and daughter-in-law occupied the room opposite hers. She had inadvertently left the velux window open and it had rained while she was out. The clothes she had left on the bed and the bedding was soaking wet. She was too embarrassed (or considerate) to call us (it was quite late) so she slept on her son's bedroom floor. I felt awful that the poor woman had slept on the floor: we could have certainly done something for her. It also made me wonder if I had not been friendly enough when she arrived, though her daughter said she was just that sort of person. I wanted to give her a cuddle to make up for her bad night.

Most guests are at their ease here. One of our guests and her niece (she is more of a friend now and is moving up this way) were doing a thunderous highland jig when Charles walked into the dining room to get the breakfast order. (We tend to play Scottish music over our sound system.)

One man we couldn't get to stay at *any* price. He'd been referred to us the same day by a nearby guesthouse. He arrived, parked his car beautifully and rang the front door bell. By the time Charles got to him (within a minute or two) he was in a lather. He said he couldn't *possibly* stay since our car park was too awkward. It is on the small side with the entrance somewhat steep. Charles was taken aback by the sheer force of his anger. The people this gentleman had just come from, across the valley, had had equally bad parking space and no doubt he was hoping for something better. Anyway, he announced he couldn't possibly sleep that night worrying about how he was going to negotiate getting out of the car park in the morning. He flew off in a rage, leaving Charles speechless. You can't win 'em all.

Actually a few guests *do* arrive bad-tempered. You have to be nice but get out of their way as quickly as possible unless you want to process their negative ions all afternoon. They take themselves upstairs, have a cup of tea and rest, after which they're fine. But meanwhile we're left with this unpleasant image of the people in the bedroom. They're fine in the morning, of course. It's odd how stressful holidays can be. Middle-aged to elderly Americans are worst at holidaying than anyone else. I can only imagine that they're so cosseted at home that they barely manage to cope with being away. Mind you, to them we're a foreign country presenting the added stress of having to drive safely on the wrong side of the road. On the other hand we do actually get charming *and* returning Americans, so some *do* cope!

Many of the guests have a certain *something* that makes one remember them. Cyril and his crowd are retired (they think they're real hell raisers) and come just one day a year on their way north on a golfing trip. This will be their tenth year. They're very jolly but do block bookings that might have stayed a few days. However, they're like old friends and we wouldn't dream of not having them. Miss Vertue comes in an erratic fashion. In fact it's time we saw her again. She is of indiscriminate age and contracted polio in India as a child, so wears leg calipers. This doesn't stop her shimming up to our second floor a good deal better than our able-bodied guests. Then there's Julie and Brian who came on holiday, liked it so much they came back and got married here; and another Julie and Stuart who did the same and we had to go to the wedding as witnesses. An amazing coincidence was that they vaguely knew another couple staying (good job they weren't marrying on the QT!) who came to the wedding and videod it. I saw a young couple one day I didn't recognize. They asked for a room 'in the roof.' I showed them up to the attic rooms. "Yes, this is the one we had last time!" they said gleefully. We don't always realize we've had repeaters till they check out. There's Mr M. who talks a lot; he talks on the stairway, he talks at the front desk, at the front door, on his way to the car, as he's putting luggage into his boot, as he's getting into the car, as he's sitting in the car with the window wound down and as he's reversing out shouting that he'll be back in a few months! There's the Chitties, a dear couple in their sixties—a handsome couple who married just a couple of years ago. He treats her with such deference and respect, yet can be quite firm. Clearly he adores her. She brings in a couple of her lovely paintings for me to see and gives me lots of tips (I paint occasionally). She even brings old painting magazines for me. That reminds me of a French lady I found sitting in our garden doing a lovely watercolor of the Abbey across the river. It was unusual and I said I'd love a copy if she ever had some done, thinking she would just think I was being polite. Well, she came back two years later with a copy. I was delighted and it hangs in our dining room (together with another painting done by a guest who presented us with *his* bright oil of the hotel).

Our 'German Drinkers' (Fred and Christiane, remember?) left us the first time to travel north. They'd hardly been gone a day when they phoned to say: 'Here are your German Drinkers!' and could they come back since they were homesick for Rosebank! People are so precious. We had a couple where the lady was disabled to the point where her husband had to push her up the stairs. They were so desperate for a room they accepted the attic room. We couldn't believe it when they phoned on their way south and asked for the same room the following week. She said she was fine once she'd got up there, as long as she didn't have to come down again till morning. Actually, the Chitties were the same. At first they didn't book for their return journey, saying they couldn't manage the second floor (it's all we had available when they wanted to return). But after they left they phoned to book the attic room after all, saying they'd rather put up with the stairs than stay elsewhere. As luck would have it we had a cancellation by the time they returned so they stayed on the first floor anyway. People say it's like coming back home. I love that.

We rely quite a lot on our repeat trade, especially in the early part of the year. It really is worth the effort to get them back, or their friends who they recommend. It can make up as much as 50% of your bed space.

It's worth bearing in mind that you'll always give better service than staff. But if you do have staff, choose them for their friendliness as much as their efficiency. Being served by a disgruntled waitress won't encourage repeat trade. If staff are friendly the guests will reciprocate making their job easier and pleasanter and should in return make for better service.

Some you remember by their voice, some not till you see them. One man may be exceptionally tall. Or a couple may be memorable because they're tiny, very polite, very clever, very talkative, the one taking over as soon as the other stops talking. There's the man with the pretty oriental wife who's very quiet. There's the really tall lanky man from the USA who's wife we have yet to hear speak. There's the 'magic man' and his wife (he does magic tricks for my sons), golfers in their many and varied forms, fishermen who gut their catch in the kitchen for me.

One could go on and on. One memory leads to another. We're very fortunate to have met so many interesting people. I only wish we had the time to get to know them better!

CHAPTER 12

From Strength to Strength: Refurbishment, Development & Expansion!

Right from the start you'll probably see things you want to change. Maybe it's just cosmetic, like a lick of paint here and there. The chances are, however, that the place will need a bit of an overhaul. It's rare to find a hotel that's in perfect condition. Ours certainly wasn't, though we didn't realize how much it needed till we'd moved in. Quite frankly, if you want to maintain quality it's essential you do something to the place *every* year. If your place isn't too large you may get away with decorating one bedroom each winter plus doing something to a portion of the public areas, like putting in new curtains or perhaps a new carpet or soft furnishings. If you don't keep up with it then it will soon get on top of you and your place will become tatty. It will get to the point where everything looks like it's wearing out at the same time. And who can afford to refurbish half a hotel in one season? At the time of writing this we're aware that our next project is to upgrade the dining room furniture.

If your trade is seasonal, then the quiet winter months will be the best time for refurbishment and development. In our first winter we put in four *en-suite* bathrooms which meant completely redecorating four rooms plus hallways and replacing carpets in six bedrooms—not to mention taking off half the roof to restructure the attic rooms in order to add the *en-suite* facilities. (The latter involved consulting an architect and obtaining planning permission.)

The next winter we redecorated another bedroom and put in a further three uPVC windows.

The following winter we did a tiny amount of decorating in our own section and replaced another four windows, as well as install a new gas fire in the residents' lounge. All the time we were also upgrading in little ways, such as providing new kettles in the bedrooms, new washing machines, toasters and cutlery. Eventually we put in gas central heating throughout. At least every year we do a certain amount of redecorating, especially in the bedrooms. It's like the Forth Bridge: as soon as one end has been painted, it's time to start again.

Each year has gone on like this. A new bed here, new curtains there. At the same time you mustn't forget yourselves. We tended to put ourselves last if repairs or upgrading in our private bedrooms or lounge wasn't absolutely essential. (When you're viewing hotels or guesthouses with a view to buying, you'll probably notice that the owners' rooms are always the most neglected—usually very tatty and quite cramped. The condition of the owners' quarters is the *real* test of how well the business is going!)

The first year we just traded to get our feet wet, so to speak. From March to November we worked very hard but realized early on (by keeping records of the number of potential bookings we lost because we didn't have *en-suite* facilities in all the bedrooms) that two *en-suite* bedrooms were far from sufficient. We were losing business since our prospective customers all wanted their own bathrooms. This need may differ in the location you're looking at. We get mainly middle-aged couples whose children have left home, are able to afford a bit more and want their creature comforts. Trade for a year to find out who your customers are, what their needs are and act accordingly.

The Tourist Board and the Enterprise Development Agency can be quite generous in helping with grants for development projects, be they for the provision of *en-suite* facilities or bedroom extensions—or, for that matter, for the building of an altogether new hotel. But don't jump the gun and start your alterations before your application for a grant is approved! We were impatient and our workmen began to knock down walls when the application was considered—and rejected because work had already begun. We were impatient because the only opportunity for making the alterations was in the winter—and time was ticking by. But the grant certainly would have helped towards all sorts of little things. So if you have the time, do approach the grant-awarding authority as soon as possible and well before you do anything. Contact your local Tourist Board or Enterprise Development Agency.

Our two family rooms were already *en-suite* which was great. This meant we only had four rooms to convert. The two first-floor rooms were easy. Room 2 simply incorporated the existing bathroom which was in the next room. We just had to close a door in and panel the whole wall and then knock a door through to the bedroom. The old public bathroom was revolting and would have to have been changed anyway. The new one looks beautiful. Room 1 was next to the public toilet so again it was easy—just a case of blocking off a door, paneling and slapping a new door through and putting in a shower and altering the position of the loo. The basin was already in the bedroom and looked fine.

We have a friend who has an old hotel in the Lake District. I think the place is Listed. She put toilets and showers in wardrobes. Talk about space being at a premium—but it worked! Knocking down walls in a Listed building is often not allowed, so think twice about buying a Listed building.

Room 2 bathroom is commented on by many guests. We put in brown marble Scanform wall panels (similar to Respatex) round the bath and up to the ceiling and fake oak paneling round the rest of the room. We added shiny brass fittings, a wooden loo seat, an old-fashioned Victorian washstand and the whole effect is sumptuous. The only thing that spoiled the bedroom was a large velux window in the sloping ceiling being the *only* source of natural light. A few months after finishing the decorating we had a window put in the front wall and now the room has a beautiful uninterrupted view of the Abbey and town. If you leave the window open at night you can hear the river tinkling by directly below. You see, sometimes it's just a matter of making the best of what you have.

Taking away the public bathroom was a blessing in more ways than one. From time to time we got the odd drip of water from the ceiling in our private lounge which was under the public bathroom. We never *could* work out where its source was. However, on one of my many nocturnal visits through the lounge to feed Bruce (the baby), I found water literally flooding through the ceiling. I raced upstairs into the public bathroom. I couldn't see a thing for steam. Someone had left the shower running (which was over the bath) with the showerhead pointing at the wall. It must have been going for a few hours, judging by the amount of water downstairs. The water, which was very hot, was making it's way down the wall and under the tiles and behind the bath, thus into our lounge. It ruined an electric fire and soaked the carpet and settee. I suppose we should have been thankful it wasn't the sewage pipe! I feel that had the shower been in someone's private bathroom they would have taken the trouble to switch it off! If your bathrooms don't have outside windows then extractor fans are a must to take the moisture and smells out.

By the way, if you're installing a new shower, make it as simple and foolproof as possible. (One of our grading officers used the more apt term: *idiot-proof!*) We have now changed every shower in the building, but until we did people often said they couldn't get hot water. They simply weren't able to obey the instructions on the shower. Some people thought they just needed to get under the shower head and turn on the water and hot water would come out immediately, not realizing they needed to run the shower for at least a minute to get the cold water out of the pipe! So be warned, you want showers—especially electric showers—with simple 'On—Off' switches. So saying, our *simple* 'On-Off' switches have been broken a few times. People turn them the wrong way and break the thread. 'On' is right, 'Off' is left—the arrows say so. Quite frankly we can't make it any plainer, yet people still have tunnel vision or preconceived conceptions when they use the showers. So, as far as possible, choose showers that are as simple and straightforward as possible, with easy to follow instructions.

The plumbing left a lot to be desired when we first arrived. The house (Victorian) is over 150 years old. The first year was agony. If certain showers were used at the same time, then all hell would break out and every pipe in the house shake and rattle! It was worse by the stairs. A guest could be forgiven for thinking a steam locomotive was about to bear down on him from the top floor. It had something to do with water pressure and a hammerhead effect. Embarrassment in one of it's purest forms. One stood there, halfway up the stairs, spread-eagled, sort of holding the wall and trying to look nonchalant, while the sound of a hundred motorbikes revved their engines behind the wall.

While on the subject of showers it might be appropriate to ask if one should place a 'No dogs allowed in shower' notice in each bedroom. We have about three dog shows in the area a year. A lot of people won't take dogs (I wonder why!) so we seem to end up with a lot. We have the same regard for these dog owners as we have for walkers! Room 4 shower was the preamble to the pipes rattling for an age. I mean, how long does it *take* to have a shower—five minutes at most for one person? We assumed the guests were having *nooky* in the shower and if the pipe noise hadn't been so embarrassing we might have envied them. However, next day we found out why it took about 45 minutes to have a shower. Have you any idea how many hairs four Irish Wolf Hounds lose when showering? It's a lot. Not to mention the smell. (Charles said the room smelt like a zoo in the morning!) Yes, we *still* take dogs. We even had a snooty cat stay. Actually, we've been lucky, for since that shower episode the only bother is the hairs they leave. Maybe we should charge since you really do have to take a lot more care when cleaning after a dog has been in the room. Seems a little unfair to the next guest. One bed had so many hairs in it there can be no doubt the dog slept with the owners. Specify that they *must* bring dog baskets with them.

It's always a good idea to find the stop tap the day you arrive. That's if you *have* one. Ours it seems was out on the pavement. We came across the key to close it the year after we arrived. The other stop-tap which cut the water off for most of the building was behind an inside wall in the children's bedroom. I believe this used to be the garden and the previous owner but one couldn't be bothered to have it moved when she built the extension (for which she didn't get planning permission—we had to get it retrospectively!) so it was sort of boarded up. This tap, apart from being behind the bedroom wall, was situated in the only place the wardrobe could go. When we had the occasional water-type emergency, then, at top speed, we had to pull the bunk beds away to the other side of the room, empty the wardrobes and pull them away from the wall and *then* attack the tap. Eventually Charles actually cut a hole in the wall *and* in the corresponding place in one of the wardrobes so at least only the bunk beds had to be moved. Fate does like it's little joke and one day, on one of our emergency tours of the nether regions of the wardrobe to the stop-tap, we found the wadding round the pipes was *soaking*. This was due to an old lead pipe about to rupture. For once we blessed the installation of a new shower, for without it being done at that moment (for that was the reason we sought out the stop tap), the boys' room would have been flooded! Eventually, at great expense, we did away with all leaking lead pipes (most of the leaks were underground in the garden and water bills were huge), and had a new stop tap put in in a sensible and accessible place. (All this goes to show that the older your building, the more refurbishment and repairs you can expect—and begs the question whether it wouldn't be more cost effective, in the long run, to build a modern, purpose-built hotel? But that may not be financially possible to begin with, of course.)

Back to refurbishment. We have two delightful attic bedrooms which, with clever manipulation of pen and ruler by our architect, took well to *en-suites*. The beds are in an 'L'-shaped alcove, and, providing you don't wake in the night and forget where you are, you won't hit your head on the sloping ceiling. The roof had to be lifted here and there but somehow it worked. (Two back dormers were built to house the shower and toilet facilities.) If you feel something looks rather impossible, then get an architect in. Architects have a totally new perspective on things.

Since we stay open quite late in the season and it gets cold up here in Scotland we found it necessary to put in central heating. Putting *en-suite* facilities into four extra bedrooms involved the installation of 3-phase electricity, which is basically Commercially rated. This is exorbitantly expensive. It cost us good money to put in the 3-phase too! It's one of those minefields you need to examine before you decide to refurbish. We told the Electricity Board they were being too harsh but they were totally unsympathetic. After crippling bills for a year we realized that gas went by our front gate. The Gas Board agreed to put gas in free of charge provided we used it. We started with a gas cooker, then a gas fire for the guests, after which our expansion flowered into full central heating which we have never regretted. We're virtually all gas now, yet our electric bill is *still* twice as much as the gas bill! We had a company called JRT look into the accounts a few years ago and as a result a man from the Electricity Board came along and said "Why didn't you *tell* us you wanted to pay less? We'd have been sympathetic!" All I got was an abusive reply to the question a few years earlier. Anyway, JRT's address is in the back.

The coal-effect gas fire in the guest lounge creates a really cozy atmosphere and the guests love it. We even get the occasional fag-end thrown on it!

When we had the central heating put in we had to have a boiler room made. At least, we needed somewhere safe to install a largish (with all it's ancillary paraphernalia it was the size of an immersion heater) boiler. We wanted a room in which to put a new gas tumble dryer so our local joiner made a sort of conservatory outside our back door. Apart from the gas boiler, this now houses two gas dryers, a filing cabinet, a book shelf, a Stag dressing table I can't bear to part with, spin dryer, wellies and the like. It was worth every penny.

Since we arrived we have had just about every window out and put in uPVC. I know it's not like the real thing but it's maintenance-free, will last for years and to our minds has been worth it. Our bedroom was the last to be done last winter. It's awful the way one has to do things for the guest accommodation all the time and never has any money left for one's own. *Make* the money, *make* the time. You deserve it. (We've heard of guest-house owners in a seaside resort who sleep on mattresses in the kitchen during the season.)

Our dining chairs were looking as though the guests were feeding them so we re-upholstered them ourselves. We had some lovely tartan left (I made a huge tartan curtain to cover an old fireplace behind a bed which now looks like a special feature), so we got a commercial stapler and put tartan on all the chairs. They look very Scottish.

We installed a commercial gas tumble dryer last year (Whirlpool) which has been fantastic and significantly cheaper to use. It has cut the drying bills by about a third. We bought it from Advanced Systems 2000 (address in back). They phoned up recently to check everything was okay. Impressed by that. Also, if you can afford it, get a commercial washing machine. The main thing is to make sure it has a fast spin and a quick wash, since you won't have time to mess about. So saying, I cleverly bought a new one recently. It said 'quick wash' as one of the programs. Only when it was plumbed in did I read the instructions to the effect that the 'quick wash' is 40 minutes and doesn't use the fast spin setting. Will I ever learn? Actually, it's not a bad idea to take out a service contract when you buy the machines since they *are* used a lot.

By the way, putting central heating in, especially if it's an old building like ours, can take a while and make a lot of mess. Organize it for the winter or your quiet season. Never mind how long the plumber *says* it will take—he'll always go over time. We chose a fellow called Ian to do the central heating since he gave us the cheapest quote, apart from being an easy-going sort of chap with an endearing smile. But as with all workmen, his men had a tendency to disappear for a few days every now and then, leaving us with gaping holes in roofs and floorboards. Ian came in one morning, having failed to turn up the day before, to say he'd had to go and do an emergency job elsewhere. His mate then came through the door proclaiming loudly that they'd had a *hell* of a night out the evening before and were so hung over they couldn't even get out of bed! The only way I can think of getting workmen to do a job on time is to have a penalty clause in your acceptance of their quote, to the effect that if they don't finish the job in the specified time they'll lose 1% or whatever of their bill for each day lost. (My mother-in-law actually locked a builder in a room once and told him if he wanted to get out and go home that evening he had to knock his way out through the wall. He was supposed to put a hole in the wall days ago for the purpose of a new extension). Always allow extra time since contractors never finish on time. Charles had to spend the whole night decorating the last bedroom before a full house descended because the workmen took a lot longer than they said they would.

If there's an extra job to be done which hasn't been quoted for, then tie the contractor down to a price and have him submit it in writing. We paid a fortune to have the 3-phase electricity put in. Had we been told how much it would cost (and the fact that it's related to much higher bills) we'd never have done it and looked in a different direction. The bill from the electrician was about £2,000 more than expected. We could have had the entire house rewired for this.

Expanding your business depends on so many factors. How big would you like to go? Would it be *profitable* to put on extra rooms (have you the space?), would you need extra staff to service the extra business? For us it has been impossible to expand due to the physical constrictions of space (we're situated on a steep river bank and there's insufficient level ground to expand). Yet, it's quite possible that our profit level wouldn't increase significantly with the addition of another four or five bedrooms. Our *turnover* would certainly increase (which would make VAT registration necessary), but not the *profit*. With additional bedrooms our overheads would increase. Our personal workload might decrease but then having staff can be as stressful as doing it yourself! Most certainly do a *cashflow* forecast before expanding. If your rooms provide accommodation for under six people (we take at least 14) then you don't pay rates, and you don't have to satisfy the Fire Regulations which can be expensive if you're just setting up. Obviously, the bigger you are the more the turnover, but that means more headaches. On the other hand, if you're after a small business to run on your own, there's only so much you can do. Just one member of staff is useful so you can have time off. I suppose my experience in hotels in the past has put me off—when I recall the minor pilfering that goes on. Friends in our position seem to have such headaches with staff—that is, if they even turn up for work. We've heard of bedrooms not being done at all. Imagine taking a guest to a room to find that it hasn't been touched since the last occupant left in the morning! Once we employed a cleaner who talked to 'spirits' on the way round. There was more talking done than working! (*And* the cleaner in question was being paid by the hour. Who said spiritualism wasn't profitable?)

See where can you improve your building without doing something useless that isn't really needed or isn't going to bring in more money. We desperately need a bigger car park. It would involve a retaining wall and landfilling, and the quotes we've had make us realize it isn't worth it since we would never recoup that money. We won't get more rooms because of a larger car park—it would just make life a lot less harassing! (Another thing: if you do expand the number of letting bedrooms, or simply start up a B & B, the Roads Department of your Local Council will want to know about it: if your car park is small, you may have a problem in getting their approval.)

So, consider the position if you managed to put in, say, an extra three bedrooms. It would mean you'd need three more tables in the dining room, six more sitting places in the lounge and space for three more cars in your car park. Can you recoup the cost reasonably quickly by the extra takings? Be careful though not to overcapitalize. Do you have a piece of land in which you could rather put up a self-catering chalet and let it as overflow if you don't let it every week to self-catering guests?

Think of other possibilities. If you're just opening a couple of rooms then consider how you're going to cope with the bathroom situation for family and guests if you're short of bathrooms!

Just a mention about Planning Permission—a somewhat thorny subject but worth bearing in mind quite early on if you're considering structural changes. The architect we employed to do the alterations for our *en-suite* facilities applied for the planning permission on our behalf. He took everything off our shoulders. However, we later bought a house to do up and sell. It also served as an overflow for a few months but had us heading headlong into VAT, not to mention the extra work load! This house had a sort of laundry room at the back so we put a shower and a loo in and didn't get Planning Permission. We didn't think it was necessary since no structural changes were involved. But it turned out we should have since when we sold it we had to get it retrospectively. It worked out all right but could have been a disaster—especially had the authorities not liked what we had done. They can make you take down your new piece of work so be careful. If it's something high profile, then you may get neighbors objecting. Even something as simple as new windows may require Planning Permission. In some conservation areas, for example, you're not allowed to take away sash windows; you have to replace them with the same type of windows you had before. When we bought our hotel the solicitor handling the purchase found there had been an extra bedroom built on the back for which there was no Planning Permission. The then owners were obliged to get Planning Permission retrospectively before the transaction could be completed. Nevertheless, the addition was very shoddily done and I feel had the Planning Permission been applied for when it was built it wouldn't have been granted.

If you're just changing the use of your house to B & B then the Local Authority will want to know. You may have to apply for a 'change of use.'

Anyway, if you're going to do it yourself then contact the local Planning Department of your local authority and they'll send someone around. They can actually be quite helpful! We bought a lovely cottage outside town. We renovated it but didn't think it was necessary to apply for Planning Permission when we replaced the rusty and leaking skylights with new double-glazed Velux windows. The Planning Authority came around as they do when they see *anything* going on, quite uninvited. They actually passed our ideas for a new door we thought would never get through and yet objected to the beautiful Velux windows! The old ones were rusting and dangerous, not to mention unsightly. Well, I said, we'd just have to put the old ones back in then, and to my surprise the man said, "Oh, never mind. I'll just note the alteration on our records!" I suppose a little give and take on both sides is required. To be safe, though, contact the planning authorities at the outset. Don't leave it to a trial and error process as we did! If you make an effort to comply and do the right thing then you're in with a chance.

We actually bought this cottage to live in ourselves, but as we were hardly there in the summer we put it in the hands of a nationwide holiday-cottage agency. This turned out to be a rip-off! The commission they charged was exorbitant. The cheques we got were not worth the effort we put into it. The agency was horribly strict about furnishings and facilities, which in turn meant a big financial outlay on our part. It would have taken us years to recoup the cost had we bought the cottage just for holiday letting with this agency. They also had a complaints questionnaire system which encouraged people to complain about such petty things as the curtains in the lounge not matching the lounge suite, the sheets not matching the bedroom curtains, the kettle lid coming all the way off instead of simply flipping back, and the shower fixture being too low (the guest who complained about this wasn't able to lift the shower-head off its cradle and hose herself by hand, in spite of including the letters 'B.A.' behind her signature!) The complaints were really *unbelievably* pathetic! The sheets were indeed the same color as the bedroom curtains, but is the fact that they don't have the same pattern of flowers (or ducks, or teddy-bears, or zigzag lines) going to destroy your holiday? I think some people just don't allow themselves the luxury of enjoying their holiday whatever the circumstances, and their neuroses are readily nurtured by the sort of questionnaires the agency provides. The agency also had a penalty clause that if we came out of the system before the specified time, then we had to pay a thousand pounds. Pay up we did—to the tune of £2,000, since we sold both our holiday properties during the period of the contract. They were quite unrelenting in their quest for this money, in spite of our having found suitable alternative accommodation for the few bookings they had made. So, in short, if you want to branch out into holiday cottages or holiday homes, I wouldn't advocate joining an agency. Remain independent and do your own advertising.

Again, with self-catering properties, be careful of your VAT threshold, since if you and your partner conjointly own your hotel *and* the self-catering unit(s), then both business are regarded as falling under the same VAT umbrella. Self-catering seems to go hand in glove with a hotel, even if the unit is on a different piece of ground with a separate title deed. (If husband and wife own the properties separately, of course, then, as sole traders, they'll have a separate VAT threshold for their respective businesses.) It's worth being aware of these pitfalls!

Also, remember that guests incur a fair amount of damage over the season—so at the least you're going to have to repair *their* damages, even if it's just chips out of the paint and gouges out of the wood due to luggage.

And finally, remember the disabled if you're building a purpose-built hotel. It makes good sense to be *accessible* to *all*. There's a distinct lack of holiday accommodation for the disabled. Ask your Tourist Board for their booklet on disabled accommodation.

CHAPTER 13

Competitors or allies?

There are quite a few B & B's and guesthouses as well as two small hotels in town—but I wouldn't exactly call them competitors since I know most of them and their owners are lovely people.

Each place is different and that's probably the reason for our lack of animosity. We ourselves are unique in that we offer food and have a small bar and all our rooms are *en-suite*. We also have a private lounge for guests and provide keys for guests so they can come and go as they please. (This doesn't stop guests getting locked out, of course. I had a party of young men wake us the other week at 2 a.m. saying they couldn't find the side door. We don't have a side door and I don't believe I ever intimated that we had.)

There are a couple of hotels in town that offer the same if not more but they are likely to attract different guests. For instance, one has karaoke evenings and has a loud bar; the other is cheaper and has a very run-down bar. Our guests wouldn't be caught dead there but then it takes all kinds. (Our kind come here and other kinds go elsewhere!) Someone actually found us rather quiet and asked if there was a noisier place in town! I wasn't offended and knew exactly where to send them.

Once a year the town has a street party and it's held on the green over the river opposite us. A live band plays *very* loud music until midnight and attracts quite a local gathering. It's the prelude to our local two week-festival. One young couple came down the first year to complain about the noise and asked if I couldn't find some way of 'making them turn the music off.' I now make a note of the date, put it on my chart and warn people when they book that it's going to be noisy.

But again, I digress. The other B & B's and hotels are friends. Instead of turning people away when we're full we phone around to find somewhere for them to stay in town. We fill one-another up. Otherwise the guests might end up going to the next town. They do the same for us so as long as we have the time we refer people to one-another and try to use a rota-type system so we don't leave anyone out. We keep copies of other establishments' brochures under our reception desk so that, once we've phoned an 'ally' to verify they have the required accommodation, we can hand the relevant brochure to the potential guest and help, if necessary, with directions. (A good brochure will always have a sketch map on the back showing location.) People are usually quite overwhelmed by this sort of friendly assistance and been very grateful. (Be sure to hand them one of your own brochures, too, in case they return to the area.)

So the message is to turn competitors into allies! Instead of competing, help one another, especially if you run out of something. Don't be mismatched, though. Don't send the queen to the local doss house and the tramp to the Hilton. They definitely won't appreciate it! (Well, the tramp might!)

Sometimes we share guests. If someone phones and wants more rooms than we have then we offer to book the extra in somewhere else. This seems to work very well.

Of course it's good to stop in the street and exchange *guest gossip* or just have a good moan. The best story ever was told by Fiona who has a beautiful Victorian guesthouse over the valley from us. She had French guests who checked in mid-afternoon and went straight to their room. At 8 p.m. they came down and asked for breakfast. Fiona thought they meant dinner. The French speak English as badly as we speak French. Fiona said she didn't do dinners but there were restaurants in town. They were somewhat aghast and said they wanted *breakfast*. Fiona tried to explain that breakfast was only served in the morning—but the Frenchman kept pointing to his watch, saying it *was* breakfast time. Then (for Fiona) the penny dropped and she had to strain to stop herself giggling. These people thought it was the next *morning*. They had obviously fallen asleep in their room and woken just before 8 p.m., thinking it was 8 a.m. and time for breakfast.

At this point Fiona couldn't stop herself and burst out laughing. The Frenchman was *not* amused and got angry as she tried her best to explain the problem. But he stood his ground and insisted it was time for *le petit dejeuner*. Eventually she gave way and served them breakfast. Satisfied, they paid their bill for bed and breakfast and went on their way. Fiona was even able to let their room again that night. (Fortunately she never heard from them again, though she was quite prepared to refund their money. To this day she wonders what they did when the sun set at 9 a.m.)

Anyway, that's how it is with competitors. Allies, I mean. You can swap stories about how stupid everyone else is and how incredibly patient, long-suffering and clever *you* are!

CHAPTER 14

Pernicious Allsorts

There are lots of miscellaneous items you need to consider when entering the hotel or hospitality trade, bearing in mind that you're acquiring your own business. Being your own boss makes you responsible for matters like insurance and fire precautions, health matters and the telephones you install. I'll talk about some of these here, but will start with the most essential matters like insurance, fire precautions and your hotel licence.

Insurance

We seemed to end up with lots of different insurance policies but eventually honed it down. When we bought our hotel the Bank which gave us our mortgage actually didn't insist on a Mortgage Protection insurance. This is apparently because it was a commercial mortgage, so you need to watch this and make sure you're fully covered.

I would recommend Mortgage Protection, Buildings Protection (cover for fire and other types of damage), Personal Property and Guest liability cover. The latter should cover employers' liability even if you don't have staff, just in case. The guest liability needs to cover at least £1,000,000. People *do* fall down stairs and do silly things to themselves (thus far not here, touch wood!). Put up a Public Disclaimer. Your insurance company should give you one with the guests' cover. It should state that you will not be held responsible for any harm coming to the guests or their belongings or loss of belongings while on your premises. A lot of firms do a hotel package which covers everything. I'll list a few names in the back but get a broker to shop around for you. It shouldn't cost you anything and he can do the legwork and tell you what it all means. It's also a good idea to take out some form of health insurance in case you have to spend time in hospital or just be laid up in bed so you can't do any business. This money should at least pay someone to do your work while you're out of action. Again, consult a reputable broker. You get what you pay for. I pay by Direct Debit so the premiums can't be forgotten. Insurance is quite expensive but I don't like to give fate a chance!

Fire Precautions

At present you're not allowed to sleep more than six people (including staff) without a Fire Certificate. This includes children. Neither are you allowed to let rooms above the first floor or below the ground floor without a Fire Certificate. So if you do consider buying a place that can take more than six but hasn't the necessary certificate then get the Fire Service to come along and tell you what will be required. It will probably involve fire doors and smoke detectors in all rooms plus hallways and emergency lighting. This can be expensive but don't try to get away with it. The guests are your responsibility and are trusting you to do the right thing by them. Never take a risk with a guest's life. A lot of people still smoke. This alone is a huge hazard.

Our first night here was eerie, sleeping in our new *attic* bedroom at the back of the building. It's actually on the first floor and I think used to be the stables! The garage was absolutely brimming with boxes to be unpacked. When you move into a hotel the cupboards are already full. Where do you put your belongings? We organized two large garden huts to be erected in the back garden the day we arrived. (We're still storing things in there.) Anyway, I slept like a log that first night but Charles didn't. He was kept awake by a slight burning smell. I'm a fire freak so he thought that if *I* was sleeping through it, it must be okay. Great! Next night, having got to bed early, *I* could smell rubber burning. Being more terrified of fire than the VAT-man I *had* to trace the source. I traced it to a huge metal box in the larder—right under our bedroom! It was making crackling noises and suffusing the air with an acrid smell. It had a seal on it with a warning that opening the box carried the penalty of death! Needless to say I slept downstairs in the lounge next to the kids' room in case we had to make a dash for it. The box was still hissing the next morning and we got the Electricity Board in pronto. Sure enough, a fat wire, the width of my thumb, had burnt out. Thinking back, we should have called the Electricity Board straight away or got the firemen out to look at it. We had no guests in and hadn't realized how bad it was.

Anyway, if you're going to accommodate more than six people, then be prepared for some expensive fire equipment. We get ours serviced once a year. An empty fire extinguisher is no use to anybody. If you do sleep less than six I would still recommend smoke alarms in hallways at least, as well as in the kitchen. Our alarm goes off if we burn the toast. In fact, it went off for no reason one day. We raced around checking all the rooms. We reached the top floor to find the culprit. The ceilings are low in places and the man in one of the attic bedrooms had knocked the whole smoke alarm off the ceiling with his head. Would you believe it, he was a fireman by trade and managed to put it back!

We also bought extra fire extinguishers. Silly to be dead or scarred for life for the sake of a few pounds. When buying a place, always check their certificate is up to date. In fact, in a going concern the sellers should give you the certificate. Keep it in a safe place. The fire authorities come round about twice a year and check you out. You'll also have to check your fire alarms and lighting once a week to make sure it works! (Our toaster checks it every day!)

Also, put a notice behind each bedroom door telling the guests to leave the hotel immediately on hearing the fire alarm and not to go back into the building, and to raise the alarm once outside. They will need to know the quickest way to the exit. Ask the Fire Officer to help you work out this notice relevant to your premises.

As an extra act of safety don't put off all lights at night. Leave landing lights on.

Telephones

Isn't it funny. They drive you up the wall and yet we can't do without them. If you take over an existing hotel or B & B from someone always take their number since it will be in their advertising and if they have goodwill, previous guests will want to phone and book. We have a small public phone in the hall for guests, connected to our private line rather than to our business line. We found it very frustrating in our first year to find guests hogging the phone during prime booking time. Most of our guests are like ET and have to *phone home* the minute they arrive. We felt we were probably losing a lot of business, for at first the payphone was plugged into our business line—so that if a guest was using the line, no bookings could come in. (And this was often around 5 p.m., just when the Tourist Information Center was likely to phone us with bookings for that night!) So we got an extra line. We call it our private line and give the number to family and friends with a warning *not* to call on the business line. We just hooked the pay phone in the hall to this new line so we *share* it with the guests. If you have children that frequent the phone then a private line is essential. We keep the business line free since it's the number used in all our advertising and, as I said, the TIC use it too.

We originally rented a payphone and I think we got totally hoodwinked (we're incredibly naive). We paid about £600 for the use of this thing and it still wasn't ours. So, for goodness sake, buy your own payphone—they're cheap enough! Look around and get one that's as simple as possible. Ours is an AGIFON 50 (address in the back). It was the simplest we could find. Foreign guests (especially from the Continent) are inclined to phone home far more frequently than British guests, so your payphone (like your electric showers!) needs to be as simple and straightforward as possible. Be sure to bank the money when you empty it, ready for the phone bill. Keep change in though, since people never seem to have any. I've heard of some people who carry their own phone around, unplug yours and plug theirs in, thus getting a free call. So try to locate the socket in your private area. We have wonderful guests and have only had a problem once when we had a crowd of young Argentineans staying. All their friends who were staying at neighboring guesthouses and B&B's came to use *our* phone. It was non-stop one evening (they were still chatting to girlfriends and wives in Argentina at 2 a.m.!) and it made us suspicious—so eventually we sent the intruders from the other B & B's away and unplugged the phone. We don't know what they were doing but our phone bill was £100 more than the money we took! We'll take the phone out before they arrive next time!

Nearly all of your business (90% easily!) will come through the phone. Develop a really greasy telephone manner! (Charles is disgustingly greasy on the phone. Maybe he's just an all-round greasy—oops, I mean charming—person!) When checking advertising proofs always check the phone number. Once we didn't get to see one set of proofs and guess what, the phone number for that ad was wrong for the whole year! (Which meant absolutely no bookings came via that ad.) We use an answer-phone in the winter when we're out but people don't like them. Better to use the facility to see where the calls have come from and phone them back. We found Call Divert really handy. Just tap in the digits BT give you and all the calls from that line will be diverted to wherever you want, even Australia (though that would cost a bit!). You pay the cost of the call from wherever your home phone is to wherever you are.

There are all sorts of different facilities nowadays. BT do a brochure. It's always worth a look to see what you're missing. A FAX machine is essential nowadays since so many guests choose to confirm their bookings this way. Nevertheless, I'm reluctant to make my FAX number public (i.e. to have it appear in my advertising) for the simple reason that you get a load of faxes requesting brochures and the like from all over the world and they rarely turn into bookings—you just run around like a chicken with its head off faxing all day, expensively!

Health Certificates

It seems strange that there are more outbreaks of food poisoning now than ever before. We have better refrigeration and stricter health control over the sale of foods than we had twenty years ago, yet more people than ever are dying from food contamination. The Health Authorities would like anyone who deals with food to take a Health & Hygiene course so they are more aware of where the dangers lie. Anyone who deals with food should have training commensurate with his/her work. It's the employer's responsibility to see that staff are trained. They can train them themselves or send them on a course. They should of course really go on a course themselves. Don't take the chance. The Health Authorities can close you down without warning if they think you're a risk. The courses are only a few hours long and are incredibly simple. It's all common sense, but I did learn a few things. There was hardly any paperwork and there was a simple multiple-choice exam at the end. It's easy and quite a good idea really, and is handy for asking questions. For instance, did you know that your fridge has to be kept at 0 to +2c for raw meat, +1 to +4c for cooked meat and that your freezer should be -18 to -21c? The course makes you more wary and with all the food poisoning going on nowadays you need to take care. It would be cheaper to do it at your local college. Phone your Health Authority and ask them to recommend one. Some people run courses privately but I wouldn't bother paying that much. It will probably be your local health official who runs the course at the local college, so you'll get to know him personally which, I'm sure you'll agree, is a very good idea. You'll also meet other folk in *the business* and you'll be able to pick their brains and see what they do that you don't!

Food areas must be clean and in a good condition. Bits of wood chipping off a worksurface would not be acceptable. Care should be taken when handling food. One shouldn't be smoking, and hands should be washed after touching meats. Bins or anything that could cause contamination should be washed. Foodstuffs should be kept in sealed containers to keep out risk of mice and insects. Bins must have lids on. There must be adequate ventilation and light. Anyone unwell should not work with foodstuffs. It's all common sense really. Ask the Health Board to send you their leaflet.

Three winters ago I did a first-aid course—just so I wouldn't feel totally useless if someone should stop breathing in front of me. A refresher would be a good idea. Again, your local Tourist Board will probably be able to tell you where to go if you fancy taking this sort of thing further. You have to keep a clean and hygienic health box on the premises at all times. I bought one from Boots and keep it under the reception and keep it just for guests. So far nobody has needed it. You should also keep a book to note any use of said box, date, name, type of wound, so if there are any repercussions you can refer to said book.

Talking about the Tourist Board. If you're new to an area and don't know where to get things, then the TIC should be able to help with lists of suppliers. Ours does.

Licence

We have a Restricted Hotel Licence. This means only residents and their guests may drink here. The resident must pay for his guests' drinks. Our licence is reassessed every three years. Sometimes you have to go to the meeting that will be held locally to check that you are still fit to have the licence. Someone will probably call round close to the meeting date and check you out. If it's a Restricted Licence, make sure you keep the drinks behind closed doors, that you don't actually have a *bar* but do this on a dispense system—i.e. you don't have optics and drink in view or have a bar counter. He will check out a few safety aspects of the hotel like electrical cords in bedrooms, on bedside lamps, kettles, etc. Make sure fire exits are accessible. The common sense sort of things. He'll also check your kitchen, larder and fridges:—the sort of food you serve and that it's kept in an hygienic manner. The Licence Board will let you know when your licence is due for renewal. It costs about £70 now! If you're required to attend the meeting you generally just have to be present while the Chairman asks various Departments—Health, Fire, etc., if there are any objections to your licence being renewed.

If you're doing this for the first time then you can ask your solicitor to go along with you or merely to represent you. He'll advise on all aspects. Abide by the rules and you're fine. (The rules are simple enough—such as displaying your prices in a public place, not watering down the drinks, keeping bottles behind closed doors, not having a bar counter, using the same measurement for all drinks, not selling alcohol to anyone under the age of 18. They'll vary according to the type of Licence for which you've applied. A Full Hotel Licence will of course have a different set of rules.)

A Licence is not transferable on sale. It must be in your own name. Some Licences have to be renewed every year. It depends on your type of Licence and your area.

With a Restricted Hotel Licence your residential guests can drink any time. This can be unfortunate, of course. Once we were woken at 2 a.m. by Mr X and his crowd, just back from the pub. Could Charles give them a corkscrew? (Yes, they woke us up for a *corkscrew*!) Charles came down in his pyjamas and gown, bleary-eyed, and handed them a corkscrew without comment. "Thanks, mate!" responded Mr X enthusiastically, and added breezily: "Oh, as long as you're here, you may as well open up and give us some drinks from the bar!" Thereafter I think they must have detected something cold in my disposition since, when they checked out, they left a card and a box of chocolates for me. They were golfers and I must admit most of our golfers seem to have an amazing resilience in regard to late nights: they can repeat these night after night yet still be down for breakfast for 8 a.m.

I think I've already mentioned that you're also supposed to display your hotel prices (i.e. tariffs) in a prominent place. This will be checked by someone official at some stage!

Purchasing

Apart from Brake Brothers (suppliers of frozen food) and Booker Food Services, we use the Cash & Carry. We'd use it more but it's a bit of a distance for us to travel and we'd only see things we didn't want and be tempted to buy. If you live near a Cash & Carry then you'll find it very handy since one can get almost anything from frozen food, sweets, beers, cheese, plates, cups, glasses, sheets, soups and numerous other things. Go along and ask for a form to fill in. They'll need details of your bank account and what business you run and most of all what limit you want to set yourself. We still have a limit of £300 per purchase which is adequate. (You can make a purchase to the extent of your limit as often as you like.) We were worried that if our limit was too huge we might go overboard. It really depends on your special circumstances. The Cash & Carry will give you a membership card and you must take it with you each time you go. It's just like going round a huge supermarket, but you buy cases of things rather than single items. (There's often a 'discount' or special offer section where you can buy half-price goods whose sell-by-date is close—often a huge bonus or temptation for your own personal pantry!)

Brake Brothers phone once a week for our order and deliver once a week. If you're in the right area and need them to call twice a week, so much the better. They have a minimum order value of £50. They cover most frozen foods. It's well worth getting their brochure. (Address in back.)

Booker Food Services or '3663' (who used to be called *Fitch's*) sell almost as much as the Cash & Carry and, like Brake Brothers, they *deliver*. They also phone once a week and deliver once a week, but this depends on your area. Again there is a minimum order of £50. Quite frankly it's all too easy to get to £50! (I prefer to use these suppliers than visit the Cash & Carry since it eliminates impulse buying: you only order what you specifically need! Furthermore, delivery is free and saves you the wear and tear on your vehicle as well as fuel costs.)

For fresh meat and vegetables I try to buy locally. This is a country area and if we don't use our little local shops we'll lose them. My local butcher is also indispensable, and he will deliver any time of day.

You'll no doubt have your own particular brand of wholesalers. We have Dunlopillow quite close and if we want to buy a decent amount of say, pillows, then they'd give us a decent price. Look in *Yellow Pages* or find a local trade journal. You'll also find people selling things locally that are of use to hotels and will send you mail-shots anyway. From time to time we get brochures through the door from trades and journals. You can actually buy whole bedrooms from some. I mean, bed, lights, dressers, wardrobe, curtains, carpets, paintings, the lot! The prices are generally very reasonable too. I'll put some addresses in the back.

It's a good idea to watch out for auction sales. Phone a few local auction houses and ask them to keep you informed of sales that would be of interest to you. You can get some good hotel equipment this way.

Lost Property

People regularly leave things. From experience I would say don't send anything on without getting payment for post and packing first. People probably have very good intentions of sending you a cheque on receipt of goods, but in practice I so rarely get the money back that I now refuse to send anything without the money first. (Unless, of course, it's a trivial amount.) We've had people leave whole dressers full of clothes. One old gent came and said it was his first time away without his wife. (She'd died the previous year.) He phoned us when he got home. "This is the silly old bugger from room 2 calling. I came home this morning with an empty suitcase. All my clothes are in your chest of drawers!" (The poor old thing was so used to his wife doing the packing it hadn't occurred to him! He paid me back of course.)

We had one couple leave a side of venison in the freezer. (This is a rather irritating habit some guests have—asking us to store things overnight in our freezers; they usually forget to ask for the stuff when they leave, and we don't always remember to remind them.) Our daughter, who was looking after the hotel at the time, had forgotten, as had the guest, and off they went next morning without it. We had to keep this huge thing for months before they came this way again. I think they were from the Orkneys. Our freezers are pretty well packed in season so this sort of thing we can well do without.

CHAPTER 15

So do I really want a small hotel?
(A few good reasons to make you think again!)

This is my *gripe or get-it-off-your chest* chapter, so if you don't want to be put off then skip it!

Owning and running a small hotel is a *lifestyle*, not a job you can forget about over the weekends, or escape from between 5 p.m. and 9 a.m. In fact, there seems to be very little private time, or even time off during the season. One has to be prepared to work from 7 a.m. to 10 p.m. (or later!) with very little time off—depending, of course, on how busy you are and how many staff you have. People assume you have *oodles* of time. One guest said after I had finished serving dinner: "Go and put your feet up now dear"—as if putting a pot of coffee in front of her meant that all the dinner dishes were washed, the dishwasher had been emptied and filled again, the dining room tidied after her, the breakfast tables set and the kitchen cleaned and ready for breakfast, the bills made out, the kids showered and in bed (having not had a bedtime story because I was doing dinner), and the laundry been ironed and put away. "Yes," I said with a wry smile, "I'll go and put my feet up!" Exhaustion is perhaps the biggest hurdle.

If you have no staff and have small children, then you can expect to have no time to yourself and not a lot for your children. I think children of hotel owners are probably the most neglected. The upside is that you're there all the time. That means, of course, you're there for everyone else's kids too!

If you want serious time off then you have to employ full time staff or find a hotel sitter. We found Denise, a wonder-woman who started as an occasional cleaner and became a friend. She is very capable and occasionally we take a day off, leave Denise in charge and go off for the day. This of course means *after* we've served breakfast and made a start on the laundry, often returning late afternoon to find people wanting dinners. Denise also gives us the odd night off if we want to go out for dinner. We look after her little boy sometimes to reciprocate. Actually, I really think you should make time to go out once a week. It does us no end of good just to get away for a few hours' peace once in a while; and to have *someone else cook for us is sublime*!

Finding time to do even little things, like visiting the loo, can be awkward if you're on your own. If it's not the phone it's the front door bell. I hope you're not a TV addict since you'll never see a program through without interruption. If there's really something you want to see then have a tape ready and record it, so you can see what you missed later!

Get out the Rennies! I once said to a friend who had joined us for dinner that we rarely get to eat a meal without interruption. His expression suggested the response, "Oh yes, don't exaggerate." Well, he was *gobsmacked* by the end of dinner! (There were at least four interruptions.) Unfortunately dinner for us comes at a time when the guests are arriving. This is partly because we have young children who get hungry and need to eat their main meal at a reasonable time. We can't eat at 10 p.m. since the kids have gone to bed and after 5 p.m. we're getting dinner ready for guests, so we have to coincide our meal with the arrival of the guests and many phone calls. I've got used to it, I suppose.

In a sense your home is under public ownership! We often feel we don't own the front of the house (where the guests reside). However, that doesn't stop our quarters feeling like Piccadilly Circus, either. People tend to come and go as they please. The door to our section is marked 'Private,' yet tradesmen walk in without hesitation, or perhaps with one precursory knock as a warning. Others just wander through as though our lounge and kitchen were a public thoroughfare. I know that if this were a private home they would ring the front door bell and *at least wait* for an answer.

Even the guests wander in at times. Privacy is at a premium. Some of our more talkative guests have even suggested they come back to the kitchen and help us wash up so the conversation can continue and we're not being held up! (We'd never get them out again!)

Your private rooms *must* be private from the guests or you've *had* it! In fact you must have a notice that reads *private* on your door. The only guests I've allowed in have been people who want to gut their fish. They generally end up giving them to us anyway, or having me cook them for dinner. For this I'm grateful since I could not gut a fish and to throw it away would mean it had died in vain! It's also rather interesting to see what a love these people have for the fish they catch (they even give them a quick kiss, *yuk*!). I don't understand peoples' passion for trying to get into our private quarters to be with us, even if it's ostensibly to help us wash up. Don't they realize holidays are for getting away from that sort of thing? We went on a six weeks' cruise last year and I never once had the desire to go to the ship's galley or wash a single item. Actually, our lady diners say how lovely it is *not* to have to cook and wash up.

Have a lock on your side of the door. We actually lock up our section at night. This is partly for the children's safety. You can't be too careful. I would never allow the children to sleep in the guests' section if there were guests in. If you have hyperactive children then you're heading for trouble since your kids need to be fairly quiet or they'll disturb the guests.

You can't go to bed when you like. Some guests sit up very late drinking, although it's up to you when you close the bar. You could just leave them with a drink and go to bed but if the fire needs to be turned off you'd have to wait. Even if the guests aren't sitting up you still need to be around, and dressed, up till about 11.30 in case they want you.

Once I ventured to go to bed at 11.30 p.m. Of course, the phone shrilled as soon as I had snuggled down. I rushed down in my nightshirt.

"Can I speak to Mr Hall?" said a woman's voice.

"Do you know which room he's in?" I asked, exasperated. He was a member of a golf party so I didn't know which room which man was in. "I'll have to go and knock on each door," I said. "Do you want me to do that?"

"Yes, that's fine" (Obviously, quite unconcerned.)

"I'll just go and put some clothes on, then," I said disgruntledly.

"Okay." (Still quite unmoved.)

So I went upstairs and slipped something on, then knocked on all the relevant bedroom doors—only to find that all the men of the party were out. One of them didn't return till breakfast next morning—I sincerely hoped *he* was the husband in question!

There was one young couple who rang the doorbell at 3 a.m. and took a room, paying in advance—the young lady (barely eighteen) scratching the bottom of her purse for her last dregs of change. We wouldn't have known they were only staying for a short while if the doorbell hadn't rung again—about an hour after they checked in. The same young man stood there as if butter wouldn't melt in his mouth.

"I've locked myself out and left my watch behind. Can I just go and get it?"

This sort of thing is unusual, yet the same week the doorbell rang at about 3 a.m. There were four young men swaying and reeling in the car park. One of their friends was too drunk to make it up the road and they wanted to negotiate a price for him to stay the night!

I think our worst *drunk* experience (they're incredibly rare, I hasten to add) was with an Australian guest who had been booked in by a local business firm. He was a respectable looking man and was taken out to a Burns Night supper. He was treated royally but wasn't able to hold his whisky.

Some men from a neighboring firm brought him back to the hotel. They had to wake us to get him in since he had lost his key. (Each guest is given a key to his room and a front door key on arrival. Remember to ask for these as they check out, and keep spares!) They told Charles he could go back to bed since they would take the man to his room.

Having left him comatose on his bed they came downstairs to leave. Before they got to the front door there was an almighty pounding from the room. The man was banging on the door and falling about shouting that he wanted to be let out. He didn't know where he was and believed he'd been kidnapped and locked in a strange room.

This noise made us spring into action. We thought he was breaking the whole room. (Inspecting the room next day revealed two large dents in the back of the door.) The other men sprang into action too. They raced back upstairs and opened the door with our passkey. Abuse was hurled at them.

"Why the *xxxxxx* did you lock me in? Where am I? What am I doing here? Can I have another whisky? Please! Just another *wee drinkie*!"

His companions came down a while later and said he had settled down and that they would go.

"Help. Help. Let me out!" Bang, bang went the door. (Repetition of the previous scene.)

By now other guests were getting curious. The men flew upstairs again. We said we'd have to call the police since we were not prepared to deal with a drunk who was obviously violent. His acquaintances were a decent sort and insisted they would sort it out. They phoned the company manager who had booked him in and sat with the drunk man till help came.

The factory manager duly arrived and sat with the drunk till 5 a.m., having satisfied himself that the man was fast asleep and wouldn't wake for a long time. We sat up all night too, just in case.

He, the drunk—though we can hardly call him that by the time we saw him at 2 p.m. when he was once again the respectable man we'd booked in the day before—eventually checked out. His parting words were: "I hope I didn't wake anyone coming in last night!" I gave him back his cigarette lighter which one of his keepers had given me the night before. I said there wasn't a guest in the hotel who wasn't oblivious to his being in the hotel.

On one occasion, since we were redecorating our own bedroom, we were all sleeping in one of the guest rooms when we were woken by a man slipping out of our bedroom door in his underpants. Charles blinked a few times, thinking it was a dream—but at length got up and went to investigate. He found the partially undressed man in the kitchen.

'Where are we?' blinked the man, dazed.

It turned out that, worse for drink, he had locked himself out of his room and couldn't remember which was his room. As a result he had wandered aimlessly around the hotel, trying various doors. Charles got the passkey and let him into his room, then returned to bed. But not altogether satisfied that things were as they should be, Charles once again went downstairs to investigate. He found Mr Y-fronts wandering about our larder. "Where are we *now*?" he asked as though they were on an expedition together. Our larder can seem like a rabbit warren to the uninitiated. Once again Charles returned him to his room.

Reminds me of one of our competitors who had a guest come into their room at night, in his birthday suit, and use their loo—then leave the room and go back to his own bed. (How did he know where their loo was, I wonder?)

I digress once more. In a hotel you don't always feel as though the whole place is yours. It's not like a private house where you can shut the front door and rub your hands with satisfaction, thinking, 'that's *it* then—peace and quiet!' You can't take the phone off the hook—unless you want to lose business. There's never a moment when you think you won't be disturbed, except in the winter perhaps. You can't wander about with a facemask on or in your old slippers. You can hardly go to the loo in peace.

The first year for us was the most difficult—getting used to the business while the children were small. We did all the work ourselves. It was exhausting. In fact, Charles got a hernia from the gardening. Buy help in if you're tired.

Other people will have different ideas about the downside of hotel ownership—but on the whole it's okay, once you get used to it! You *must*, however, take time off when it's quiet to recharge your batteries. If we had a different business we couldn't have taken our six weeks' cruise across the world last year followed by a three-week trek across Australia. What employer or other business is going to give you nine weeks off? The guests aside and having to be at the helm almost constantly, the best benefits are certainly the long vacations. I remember a teacher saying the three reasons he became a teacher were: June, July and August. For us it has to be November, December, and January—*and* most of February and March, for that matter!

You *will* get complaints. It's the nature of people and the nature of statistics. Thank God we haven't had many (three in fact!). Although so many of our guests are highly complimentary, complaints always feel like a personal insult! On the three occasions we've had complaints the complainers have always made *a list*. This is intriguing. Were they so infuriated by *one* thing that it led to another and *another*—or were they just hoping for a refund? One man actually wrote his list out and handed it to me, horrified to find *I* was the owner. I asked him to step into the lounge so we could *discuss* his complaints. It appeared a bee had got into his bedroom during the night (I didn't realize we had night-time bees in Scotland!). He got a *bee under his bonnet* about our not having fly screens on the window (he was Australian). He went on and on about it. This led to the bed being too hard, there being not enough pillows (he should have looked in the wardrobe for the spares), and a number of other lesser matters. Another lady coincidentally slept in the same room at a different time, and having left wrote a long letter to say she'd been horrified by seeing *drawing pins* holding up the wallpaper. She was right! There were about four drawing pins holding up the wallpaper in a corner! She was our last guest of the season and had been on a short break with us. We had noticed the wallpaper coming adrift and the glue wouldn't hold it so we thought we were being very clever using drawing pins as an interim measure. It was just for a day or two till the glue hardened. (We used polystyrene on the wall behind the paper to make the room warmer—a substance to which the wallpaper needs more persuasion than usual to stick!) Anyway, the point is this single item was the prelude to the long list of complaints which she had identified. One was that our meal was not large enough for her. (In fairness, she was an extra-large woman, though most of our diners walk through to the lounge after dinner clutching their stomachs and groaning from overeating!) I can't remember her other complaints since they were less earth-shattering than the drawing pins. (She ended up saying what lovely people we were, in spite of everything. Bless her!) The last letter was from an irate woman whose husband spent more time in my company than in hers. Enough said! (Although she, too, resorted to a list.)

You can tell those three complainers got on my nerves, can't you? Naturally you should take note of complaints that are sensible and act on them. The silly ones should waft gently over your head and out of the window. Unfortunately they *don't*—they rankle far more than the realistic, constructive ones!

If you don't like people, then don't look for a small hotel! Certainly we get fed up at times. But when all's said and done, there *are* many times when we look at others who 'work for a living' and thank our lucky stars we're here.

CHAPTER 16

The Ideal Hotel

This is our version of the ideal hotel:

All rooms will be family rooms to provide for maximum flexibility—i.e. two double beds and at least one single bed. There should be enough room to swing a cat when all the furniture is in. All rooms will be exactly the same and facing the same view. They would also all be on the *ground* floor.

The bathrooms must be equipped for the disabled with room to manoeuvre a wheelchair. This should make the facilities suitable for over half of our usual guests who *think* they are disabled as well as cater for the people with genuine needs. The bedrooms should also be wheelchair-friendly, as should the accessories. The bathrooms should be large and without tiles that get grubby. (Skanform or Respatex wall panels should be used in lieu of tiles.) All appliances should be simple to use.

There should be *generous parking* and the *spacious carpark* should be on *flat* or level ground.

I would have a large dining room which I can lease off to someone who loves doing food, including the breakfast. Then, if I chose to do so, I could run the hotel as a motel, thus cutting down on staff problems and overheads and cooking.

I would have *huge* owners' accommodation with at least three bedrooms (assuming I had a family consisting of two children)! The owners' accommodation is often non-existent in hotels, or very minute—usually a small flat.

I wouldn't have too many gadgets. The more you have the more can go wrong.

I would be tempted to make the place large enough to warrant employing a full-time receptionist. (Maybe I should just retire!)

The ideal guest you can't arrange. Theoretically, at least, the perfect hotel you *can* arrange—plan and build—bearing in mind, of course, that you can't please all people all of the time!

Here's a ground-floor plan of the ideal hotel we have envisaged. It would be ideal in an attractive log-chalet style. From the air it would resemble an aeroplane! The wings are the bedrooms. (You can extend these—add on bedrooms—when you've saved more money!) The tail-plane constitutes your private living area. The public rooms, with the kitchen at the rear (near the owners' accommodation) constitute the fuselage. We never got round to building it. Perhaps *you* will. Start by looking for a spacious piece of ground in a level area, bearing in mind the importance of location. Then apply for outline planning permission. Then approach a grant-awarding body!

SEE FIG 2 FOR DRAWING AND GROUND-FLOOR PLAN

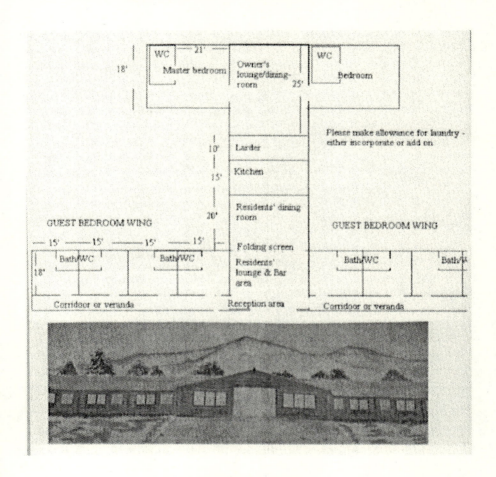

Fig 2: The ideal hotel?!

CHAPTER 17

Typical seven days!

So what's it *like* running a small hotel? Perhaps the following breakdown will give you the feel of what it's like. Perhaps it's not altogether typical, though. It's possible one's memory plays tricks on one, lumping together all the most memorable (and therfore possibly most unpleasant!) experiences. So I hope the following impressions don't put you off. Remember, they still constitute a lifestyle that's far superior to working for someone else!

Monday, 1st August

Two young golfers arrived at 9 a.m. (!) to check in. (Some of the guests were still in the dining room finishing breakfast.) I told the young men their room (room 6) was not ready for occupation. It would be in a mess—the beds hadn't been changed, the bathroom not cleaned. They didn't mind. They just wanted to get unpacked. They duly went upstairs and came down about 10 a.m. saying they were off and that when they returned in half an hour could I have the room ready for them? (I had reserved their golf in the hope it would keep them out for the rest of the day!)

The TIC (Tourist Information Center) phoned. Reserved a room for Mr Rodgers. Can he come a day early? (They said he was booked in for tomorrow. He's actually booked in for next *week*. Anyway, yes, send him up.)

Tuesday, 2nd August

Room 6. The golfers came down at 7.30 a.m. asking for breakfast. They had forgotten to arrange an early breakfast before they went to bed. They must think we use *ESP*. Could they please move to another room with a view of the Abbey? So I moved their luggage to room 4 and cleaned their old room ready for letting again. This is a four-day booking. Will they make it, I ask myself? They don't look as though they'll cope very well away from home.

The Richardsons turned up, having booked two rooms a month ago for themselves and their friends. Their friends couldn't make it. It would have been nice of them to have let us know their friends couldn't come *before* they arrived, such as when they found out they couldn't come. (I could have had their room let by now!)

Two young couples arrived in pouring rain. Happy young Germans. They managed to negotiate a keen price with me. (How *did* they do it?) Where could they put their car? Oh God, the usual question. I'll go and have a look. Good heavens—I *had* to go and get my camera! Sitting in the entrance to our driveway was a brilliant red Morgan. No roof, of course, and it's pouring with rain. Sprouting out of the two seats is the most amazing sight: two young eccentric airmen sheltering under a huge white umbrella. I wondered if they kept the umbrella up when driving. They were wearing flying jackets, flying hats, flying goggles, one even sporting a gigantic handlebar moustache. The other was very good-looking in a suave sort of way. Well, what could we do but take our car out of the garage and let them use it. The young ladies were traveling in a super BMW keeping dry. I'm still not sure who was the most sensible.

The TIC kindly filled our last few rooms with quiet unassuming people. I really like unassuming and colorless people. They're less demanding.

Would you believe it! A really old couple from Zimbabwe rang the bell. We had no room left. He *refused* to go any further. We offered to phone other B & B's but he said "I'm *not* moving again today!" What is one supposed to do? There's a triangle of grass and trees just up the *cul-de-sac* across the road. They said they'd spent many nights under the stars and would camp there! We gave them a snack in the dining room and a key for our private door should they need a bathroom. Told them to come and have breakfast after 9 a.m. in the morning when there was a free table. So, they spent the night under a tarpaulin slung between their van and the trees. Good job it stopped raining.

Wednesday, 3rd August

The Germans asked for a morning wake-up call at 7 a.m. so I had to get up early to do so. At 9.15 a.m. they're *still* in the dining room, smoking heavily and playing board games (we leave games in the guest lounge for anyone to use; some men had a whale of a time one night playing with my son's animal dominoes). I suppose they'll go eventually.

Room 2 were supposed to leave today. They haven't gone but didn't say anything and have disappeared. I need their room tonight. It's the only one with a bath as well as a shower and has been booked. I had to move their luggage upstairs and hope they didn't mind. What a carry-on! I had packed their belongings (knickers, the lot), yanked it all upstairs to the second floor, or nearly all, and while going down for the last lot I heard talking in the hallway. Oh hell, they've come back! They must have gone to town for something before returning to check out. *Sugar,* and I'd moved nearly all their things! I nimbly dashed back upstairs to retrieve their things. They came upstairs as I rushed down with their things on hangers. No, they passed me going to *another* room. Oh, no, it wasn't them after all! Back upstairs with the hangers. Well, their things eventually found a new home in the attic room. I hope they don't mind being in a smaller room with twin beds.

Very strange looking couple in room 3!

I didn't *believe* it! The two young golfers came back at 3 p.m. One had just phoned his girlfriend (from the golf course of course!) and she's sick! He must go home immediately. (More likely he can't take the Scottish rain!) He asked for a refund. Meantime I had *cleaned* their room, given them clean towels, a new tea tray, made beds and hoovered. I put on my best *landlady miffed* face and said I'd think about it while they packed. They left at 4 p.m., having showered and used the clean towels *and* had a cup of tea, messing grass all over the place. Yet they expected a refund! I eventually found the energy to do the room up later and let it to a pleasant, very smart young couple. I think she must be an airhostess. Immaculately dressed.

This morning was so *funny.* (Reminded me of a time when a young friend of ours stayed in our 'chalet'- a garden hut with a bed in it—in the back garden. My daughter had a young female friend staying there at the time. We didn't know our young friend had stayed the night and I suppose was trying to keep my daughter's friend's honor intact. I just happened to be at the lounge window folding some sheets when he tippy-toed past. He didn't see me but bumped into Charles outside the dining room window at the front. Talk about bad luck!) Anyway, the other young men had secreted a young lady in the previous evening. I was on the small landing re-hanging a picture and when I looked around I saw these young men creeping down the stairs with the young lady. They looked so covert! She even had her collar up. I wished I'd had a camera. I couldn't resist a bright

'Good morning!' What big eyes they had! They met Charles at the bottom of the stairs, too. Most of our guests are middle aged so we don't get a lot of this sort of thing.

The couple whose luggage I moved arrived back late. They weren't at all annoyed and were in fact relieved. It had only occurred to them both as they were driving back from a lovely day out that they hadn't asked if they could stay an extra day. They expected to find their luggage on the doorstep.

Thursday, 4th August

The smart young couple look quite different this morning. She's totally without makeup and thus looks about 13 and is covered in spots. Chickenpox, she thinks. She phoned her mother in tears. *Go, please go*, is all I can think. (Have I had Chickenpox?) I suggest a visit to the doctor and then back home to bed. Sounded good to them so 'goodbye'.

The rugby crowd we were expecting turned up at 10.30 a.m. What's *wrong* with people? I only had two rooms ready. They arrived back late in the afternoon begging a bucket and cloth. One of them had been sick in the taxi. I hope they don't drink any more today!

A very tall Norwegian arrived hoping for a room. He'd got off the bus to Edinburgh prematurely and the local Church of Scotland minister recommended he come to us. We were full and sent him up the road to Mrs Clark's B & B. He came back. She's full too, he said dolefully. We sent him elsewhere but he came back *again*. (Why was it *our* responsibility to look after him—because the minister said we were 'nice people,' apparently!) So, what are *we* supposed to do? He asked if he could sleep in the guests' lounge. Certainly not—what would the other guests say! The ball was clearly in our court. In the end we showed him our *garden hut* which was quite large and had been carpeted and now had bunk beds in. It was overflow storage. Yes, he was *delighted. Anything* but the hard pavement. The reason he couldn't just travel on and find a place in the next town was that he didn't have a car. Says he got off the bus here thinking it was Edinburgh! How anyone could mistake this backwater for Edinburgh is a mystery to me. We laid out an electric cable to the garden hut and left him to it. He woke us at 6.30 a.m. so he could have a shave and generally monopolize our private bathroom for the next hour. We gave him some breakfast and off he went. We got a long letter from him months later from Norway, thanking us for helping, and inviting us to visit him in his one-bedroomed flat on the tenth floor.

Friday, 5th August

Another four golfers arrived at 11.30 a.m. *Ye gods*—have these people *never* stayed in hotels before! The one who was sick is still in bed. I thought I'd leave him as long as I could. He'll just have to go. Hope he hasn't been sick again! These golfers said that we came highly recommended. We're full next week with the people who recommended them. I don't even remember the name. I suppose the faces will be familiar when we see them. Better treat their friends extra well, I suppose. Could they have tea and sandwiches in the lounge? (Can't they see I'm trying to get the bedrooms ready?)

Saturday, 6th August

A sweet American couple arrived and asked what time the shops closed, and where could they get married? *Surely* not! A pregnant pause before I replied. No, they weren't going down to the shops to get married. It transpired that this was *almost* true. They'd come all the way from the States to get wed. They're going home in four days. Not 100% about the laws but I think there's something about a couple of week's notice to be given and banns to be displayed in public. Sent them down to the pub to speak to the locals. *They* should know.

Room 2 arrived 10.30 a.m. Okay, I give *in!* From now on *everyone*'s going to arrive before lunch. They'll have to wait. My small son Bruce is having a bath. We only have a shower in our private bathroom and a bath is fun for a little boy. I can hardly check the guests into their room with an eight-year old sploshing about in their bath. They leave their luggage and are happy to take the key and come back *when I've finished the room*!

Sunday, 7th August

Room 3 can't operate the shower. This is *so* tedious. Charles goes to the room to sort out the problem. This is actually an intelligence test we put all the guests through! The wife lies naked under sheets while Charles demonstrates how to turn the dial up and down the numbers. Number one is cold and number ten is hot. Turn water on to number five and wait thirty seconds. *There* you are sir! Last week we paid the plumber £45 just to come and turn a shower off. We were in the middle of breakfast and in a dreadful rush when told by an elderly couple the shower wouldn't turn off. We rashly called the plumber since it sounded like a plumber's job. But they had simply turned the knob the *wrong* way! Talk about hitting your head against a brick wall.

Room 4 has 'congratulations on your marriage' cards strewn around (and some lovely lacy black garters). They do indeed have to wait a couple of weeks before they can marry. Shame. They're going to feel silly going home Stateside still single.

This is going *too* far! That awful man is back yet again. I remembered him when he turned up the previous week even though it was five years since his first visit. He likes to stay here because he's such a show-off and a fusspot. He should have been staying at the Hilton but then he couldn't show off since everyone there has more money than he and, looking like a tramp as he does, he would hardly have blended in. He turned up last week for *two* nights. He had such a wonderful time keeping me talking (actually, *he* did the talking) that he wanted to come back this week. I should have said we were full. He likes it so much he's turned up at 8 a.m. for breakfast, though he's not due to check in till the afternoon. Maybe I could charge him an extra day.

That rather untidy man from room 3 came down at 10 a.m. for his breakfast. He had obviously slept in his creased, dirty off-white shirt. I won't say what nationality he is but I also have it in my genes and we are known for being balmy. He's a huge man and one not to be trifled with, so I gave way and made him coffee and toast. I think he thought he'd get the works by looking mean and spotty and puffing his chest up to look taller. Well, it didn't work! Anyway, his friend who had been down at 8 a.m. for his breakfast was still sitting there so at least he had company. He stayed before and I suppose he got away with it then. I've learnt to get into *landlady mode*—hands on hips, eyes squinting, nose flaring, *you* know.

CONCLUSIONS

So, was that encouraging or discouraging?!

As with any business you go into you need to assess whether it's right for *you*. I hope my frankness in showing some of hotel life's idiosyncrasies will have given you a perspective that's clear enough to help you decide whether a small hotel is something you really want—though I trust it won't put you off at the outset! But I think you'll agree that a realistic picture *is* important. I've read of hotel owners who finish their chores and go out for the day from midday till about 5 p.m. I found that as wife and mother (striving for a bit of independence), and as housekeeper and general busybody, that such luxuries are not mine. I can only assume these people didn't have children—and worked wonderfully well together!

Really, I hope I *haven't* put you off and instead have enlightened you—so when you say '*that's* a new one!' you can laugh, knowing that it's *not* usual and that there'll be another novel situation tomorrow. The permutation of idiosyncrasies will amaze you! I hope I've made running a small hotel, or Guest House, or B & B, look easy—for really, it isn't difficult in itself. If you're organized, it's just the exhaustion (and the odd barmy guest) that gets you down!

We can't watch Fawlty Towers any more. It's too close to the bone. We find ourselves sitting rigid, like a block of ice. Where others might roar with laughter we slap ourselves on the forehead and say: 'Oh God, *yes, yes*! It's *just* like that!' If you look closely you'll see it isn't *actually* Basil Fawlty who's certifiable—it's everyone else who's *driving* him mad!

I think our motto should be 'Don't let it get to you!' Dealing with the public on such an intimate level every day can be exhausting if you let it. Quite frankly, I'm pleased to see the back of the last guest at the end of the season. I'll smile again in March when the first of the flood comes back. Until then, 'Leave me alone!' In the meantime I'm still recovering from my fortnight's overdose of sun and sand in Barbados, and sleeping in late, snuggling into the warmth under my duvet while I listen to others sliding and nudging through the layers of snow and ice outside. At least *I* don't have a boss to appease!

About the Author

Joanne at the helm!

Carolyn Joanne Muller was educated at Frenchgate Independent School for Girls in Richmond, Yorkshire. She has written for *Cosmopolitan* and *Fair Lady*, and is author of two romantic novels—*Rapture at Sea*, based on the return of Christ, and *Spirit of Ecstasy*, based on computer dating (both published by Writers Club Press). She has traveled extensively and for eleven years ran her own hotel in Scotland. In 2001 she and her husband moved to the Scottish Highlands where she runs the successful Internet accommodation guide Travel Accommodation U.K. (*www.travelaccommodation.co.uk*).

Appendix

USEFUL ADDRESSES

HOTEL ESTATE AGENTS

Christie & Co
HQ, 50 Victoria Street
London SW1 0NW
0171 227 0700

Robert Barry & Co
7 Upper Grosvenor Street
Mayfair
London W1X 9PA
0171 491 3026

On the web:
www.buyahotel.co.uk

ADVERTISING

A A Publishing
Advertising Design & Production
The Automobile Association
Fanum House

Basingstoke RG21 4EA
01256 491545

AA Hotel Services—General 01256 491647

English Tourist Board
Thames Tower
Black's Road
Hammersmith
London W6 9EL
0181 8469000

Scottish Tourist Board
23 Ravelston Terrace
Edinburgh EH4 3EU
0131 332 2433

Quality Assurance
Scottish Tourist Board
Thistle House
Beechwood Park North
Inverness IV2 3ED 01463 716996

Stilwells' Britain (Bed & Breakfast. Cheaper type of book but worth considering)
Stilwell Publishing
59 Charlotte Road
Shoreditch
London EC2A 3QT
0171 739 7179

The Lady Magazine
39-40 Bedford Street
Strand
London WC2E 9ER
0171 379 4717

Sentries (A directory for business users of medium prices accommodation)
Offwell
Honiton
Devon EX14 9SL

Yellow Pages Sales Ltd
Directories House
50 Wellington Stret
Slough
SL1 1YL
01753 553311

National Club Golfer
St Andrews Publishing Ltd
Concept House
Brooke Street
Cleckheaton BD19 3RR
01274 851323

Voucher holiday scheme:
Romin' Holidays/Discover Britain
2-4 Trinity Street
Worcester WR1 2PW
01905 613746

Brochures:

Martin Perry Publishing
48 Earlsway
Curzon Park
Chester CH4 8AZ
01244 671888

Interprint Ltd
Market Flat Lane
Scotton
Knaresborough
N Yorkshire HG5 9JA
01423 868011 (did our postcards)

Photostickers
Quick Imaging Center
131 Flaxley Road
Stechford
Birmingham B33 9HQ
0121 784 8833 (print small stickers on photos for brochures)

Stick on address labels & letterheads
Able Labels
Steepleprint Ltd
Earls Barton
Northampton NN6 OLS
01604 810781

FURNITURE & EQUIPMENT

Bedding & towells
Mushbury Fabrica Ltd
Middle Mill
Wavel Works
Holcombe Road
Helmshore
Rossendale BB4 4NF
01706 212613

Textiles, bedding, towells
Western Textiles
Regent House
Whitewalls Industrial Estate
Colne BB8 8LJ
01282 861350 (we got our top sheets made here)

Bedding, beds, kettles, luggage racks, vacume, chairs & lots more
International Hotel Supply Ltd
Unit C & D
Brunel Park
Bumpers Farm
Chippenham SN14 6NQ
0800 371184

Whole bedrooms from beds to curtains
Allied Wholesale
Willow Hall Farm
Willow Hall Lane
Thorney

Peterborough PE6 0QN
01733 223949

Bedrooms, furniture general
Barnet & Co Ltd
1291 Dumbarton Road
Glasgow G14 9UY
0141 950 1555

Luggage racks
Leaman & Thomson Ltd
11 Toberargan Road
Pitlochry PH16 5HG
01796 3483

Commercial microwave
Menumaster Europe
Unit A4
Frogmore Ind Estate
Motherwell Way
West Thurrock RM16 1XD
01708 890788

Commercial laundry & catering
Ardee Automatics
27 Tollpark Place
Wardpark East
Cumbernaud G68 0LN
01236 734441

Laundry & catering (got a good gas drier here)
Advanced Systems 2000 Ltd
Advance House
Thorn Tree Street
Kings Cross
Halifax HX1 3PH
01422 330240

Kitchen equipment
Lovat's
33 West Bowling Green Street
Edinburgh EH6 5NX
0131 555 3200

Catering auctions
Arthur Johnson & Sons
The Nottingham AuctionCentre
Meadow Lane
Nottingham NG2 3E7
0115 9869128

FOOD

Brake Bros Ltd
Head Quarters
Ashford
Kent TN25 4AG
01233 206000

Bookers Foodservice Group
Buckingham Ct
Kingsmead Business Park
London Road
High Wycombe HP11 1JJ 0194 555900

IN TRADE MAGAZINES

Free Intrade Mags:

Scottish Caterer
Bergius House
Clifton Street
Glasgow G3 7LA
0141 331 1022

Scottish Licenced Trade News—as above

Free House
 P O Box 482
Slough SL1 1HA
01753 811911

Licensee—Morning Advertiser—as above

Hotel & Rest Mag
Quantum Publishing
29/31 Lower Coombe Street
Croydon CR9 1LX
0181 681 2099

This does have subs but if you can satisfy them you have a catering business, then you should get it for free.

MISCELLANEOUS

Insurance
Commercial Union Assurance Co
St Helen's
1 Undershaft
London EC3P 3DQ   (Do hotel package)

After-sales service contracts
Service National Homecare
Darlston Road
Kings Hill
Wednesbury WS10 7TE
0121 526 4141

Legal

Music Licences:

Performing Rights Soc Ltd
3 Rothesay Place
Edinburgh EH3 7SL
0131 226 5320

Phonographic Performance Ltd
Ganton House
14-22 Ganton Street
London W1V 11B

0171 427 0311

Misc: Specialists in money saving products and services.
JRT Assoc (Europe) Ltd
Ivydene
Church Common
Semley
Wilts SO7 9AU
01747 828935   (helped with our electric account)

Printed in the United Kingdom
by Lightning Source UK Ltd.
105013UKS00001B/373